SOUL CREATIONS

Designing Exceptional Customer Experiences and Heart-Centric Worthy Lives

JOHNNY SFEIR

BE ALWAYS AMAZING!

johnny
sfeir karam

978-1-7369692-0-5 - PRINT

978-1-7369692-1-2 - EBOOK

To my wife, Vanessa. Thank you for showing me the power of belief and love, and for patiently listening to every idea and story. I could not have finished this book without your brilliant positivity, hope, and inspiration.

Contents

Who Am I & Who Are You?   vii

1. Discover Your Hospitality Style   1
2. Your Associates Are the Heartbeat of Your Organization   16
3. Handle the No-Nos   32
4. Hire and Prepare Your Team   44
5. Customer Experience Begins with a Harmonious Team   68
6. Deliver a Performance Customers Will Never Forget   80
7. Burst through Your Hesitation   114
8. Learn What It Takes to Make Your Customers Happy   134
9. HYPE-HOP Your Way through Customer Experience Design   152
10. Hope   168

About the Author   177
Before You Go   181
Acknowledgments   183

Who Am I & Who Are You?

Who Are You?

Have you asked yourself who you are? It's not so much what you have or what you have achieved. It's about who you are deep within your soul. It's about your special self, the unique you that only you can be. This is the you that others will experience, the you that extends from your authentic self in your personal life and carries over into your business life.

Whether you realize this fact or not, this is the truth. I'll show you why, again and again, throughout the many real-life stories I share in this book. All of your unique experiences will indeed become the beautiful tapestry of customer experiences only you could create. I'll be your guide to help you realize the soul creations you were *meant to create*!

Who Am I?

I help leaders design the experience that makes their lives and the lives of others worthy, whether in their business, their life, or both.

Discover Your Hospitality Style

All professionals have a specific hospitality style, whether they are aware of it or not. This is especially true for professionals in the customer experience industry.

But what exactly is hospitality style? Hospitality style is defined by several elements: who you are, what you offer, what you believe, your principles, your values, your leadership, your management style, and so on. Combined, these are what make your unique style.

For many successful companies, hospitality style is defined by a commitment to principles and service values that set the tone for the entire organization. I refer to this as style because after implementation it becomes their way of doing things and what sets them apart—their hospitality style.

Today it is more important than ever to adapt to new styles when serving customers and hiring and training associates. Failure to do so results in increased turnover, loss of impact as your reputation suffers, and customers who were previously loyal to the brand looking elsewhere for a more novel experience.

There are ten actions any organization should take to stay at the forefront and remain stylish:

- Look to the details that make the difference.
- Listen and observe to personalize and exceed expectations.
- Envision and create excellent service.
- Innovate to maintain success.
- Continue learning for growth and to fill knowledge gaps.
- Build trust to be empowered.
- Be proactive in creating both first and last impressions.
- Adapt your service culture to match the hospitality style without sacrificing its essence.
- Always be prepared to deliver an outstanding customer experience.
- Model the leadership style behind the scenes to be an example of the service culture.

All of the above are based on what I refer to as the three secret elements: *functionality, simplicity,* and *authenticity.* I call them secrets because rarely have I ever heard a leader mention these, despite the success I have seen them produce for my projects and clients.

I'll give you one more example to further illustrate this concept. You've checked into a hotel after a red-eye flight and spent the day in your destination city, attempting to ward off the ever-increasing jet lag. When you return to your room, tired and ready for bed, you realize they missed your turndown service.

The bed is decorated with an assortment of six different throw pillows, none of which have an apparent space to be stored so you can sleep comfortably. After spending twenty minutes trying to find a good spot to deposit these extra pillows, you end up throwing them on the floor. And believe me, you would not be the first to do such a thing. If this room were appointed with the three secret elements in mind, functionality would dictate fewer decorative pillows or none at all. Simplicity would include the ability to jump into bed without first having to deal with said pillows. Authenticity would speak to the quality of bedding and decor, but also not missing turndown service in the first place.

Examples of Great Hospitality Style

Now that you have a clear idea of what the three secret elements mean, let's see examples from successful organizations and how they have defined their hospitality style and its relation to the elements mentioned earlier.

Disney

Disney's four-pillar credo defines the company's hospitality style:

- Dream
- Believe
- Dare
- Do

Throughout history, a wealth of achievements have been accomplished through these same principles, which I call the Disney style.

For example, President John F. Kennedy was a man of vision and big dreams. Because of this and what he believed to be possible, he dared to make a difference in the world. The fact that he made it happen made him a doer. And there are thousands more leaders worldwide who are inspired by the Disney style, and are embracing the four principles in how they show up and serve.

Personally, I used the Disney style when it came to writing this book. I dreamed about writing a book on how to become a customer experience designer. I believed in the value I could give, and that I could help leaders in the hospitality industry take their companies to the next level through enhanced customer experience. I dared to create something different and express my approach and become a storyteller despite not having any book publishing knowledge or writing expertise. And finally, I made it happen by following through and doing it.

The Ritz-Carlton

The second company I would like to share with you is the Ritz-Carlton, which has elevated their brand to become a gold standard for customer experience at their luxury hotels and properties worldwide. The following principles make up their hospitality style:

- Define and refine.
- Empower through trust.
- It's not about you.
- Deliver wow!
- Leave a lasting footprint.

Ritz-Carlton has mastered their hospitality style. Companies and consultants across the globe have attempted to copy that signature Ritz-Carlton culture, but the Ritz will always be the Ritz. They live and breathe their unique style as only they can do, and remain at the top of their game in achieving customer experience excellence. This is of course due to the culture they've created, but can also be attributed to the three secret elements we explored earlier.

They make the experience functional and simple for the guest, and they are authentic with the quality of their service. At the Ritz, everything is possible, and this is why we consistently see them used as an example for business and leadership case studies.

Singapore Changi Airport

The third organization I've selected as an example is Changi Airport in Singapore. It is one of the world's busiest airports, with fifty million visitors each year. Voted the World's Best Airport for the eighth consecutive year in 2020, it is a model of a high-level hospitality style.

It adheres to a mission to engage travelers in a two-way dialogue in order to improve airport experiences and journeys. Customer service agents are engaged, aiming to continuously deliver an experience that is personalized, stress-free, and surprising in a positive way for all. The Changi Insiders community is highly prepared to deliver the best service and empowered to leverage their own style and personality to enhance their customer experience continually.

From a customer perspective, the design of the airport is such that instead of being bored during a long layover and resorting to fast food for entertainment, you have multiple traditional, authentic attractions to enjoy, at no added cost. Trust me, these experiences are so meaningful that I make it a priority to schedule my flights in and out of Changi Airport with the maximum layover time available. I suggest you do the same should you connect through Singapore.

Entertainments include:

- A butterfly garden located in the center of the airport
- Excursions to Chinatown and the Marina Bay Sands
- A movie theater
- High-speed internet
- Digital devices available for loan for those not traveling with them

- An exhibition of local ceramic art
- An outdoor cactus garden
- A Balinese swimming pool for the jet-lagged

Yet with all these diversions specifically designed to delight, the best part of the experience remains the people—the Changi Insiders and their approachable style and dedication to serving travelers. Employees are committed to the service values of the company—positively surprising, stress-free, and personalized— and their work is guided by these principles:

- Being positively surprising to create memories for every traveler
- Being involved
- Being enthusiastic
- Being creative

The first, positively surprising, is based on functionality. Changi Insiders make themselves available to help. Have you ever attempted to get directions from an employee of the Miami Airport? There they might send you to the wrong terminal or look at you as though you had two heads and might be capable of some wrongdoing. I travel frequently and have had many delays and missed flights and passed through many airports. Nowhere else have I witnessed the functional facilities in service at the same level as at Changi Airport. The employees create stress-free environments to provide travelers with peace of mind by:

- Being knowledgeable

- Being resourceful

- Being responsive

The stress-free environment is based on simplicity. In Singapore, they make it simple for travelers by having someone on staff available to help with any need or demand. They also speak many different languages in order to serve different countries and cultures. By doing this, they are able to attend to travelers in their own language, making the customer experience an example of ease and excellence.

The employees personalize the customer experience, because every traveler is unique, by:

- Being welcoming

- Being interested

- Being attentive

Personalization is based on authenticity. The Changi Insiders prioritize being of service. They are committed to making you feel welcome, and are attentive to every detail, maintaining authenticity in every service provided. Even at customs and immigration, you're greeted with a smile.

Changi Airport makes arrivals and departures special with smiling employees who create an outstanding first and last impression. The airport makes their nation shine at every touch-point through their delivery of customer experience excellence. The leadership behind the scenes is what makes the difference. Clear role-modeling, regular training for all staff, and rewards programs ensure that this airport continues to be at the top of its game.

Above, I have highlighted Changi Airport's hospitality style steps. Every aspect of that airport is functional and innovative, with plenty to entertain. This is an airport that helps you accept an unexpected delay with ease, and dare I say even enjoyment, owing to the positive experience while being surrounded by a high level of service excellence. Everything is simple, allowing travelers to skip the stress. Airport staff stay on top of all that happens within their territory, creating authenticity through their attitude and willingness to serve.

This is the kind of dedication to customer service that every company needs to emulate in order to excel. It's the place to visit to learn and observe how they are consistent with service, how the staff is well trained, and how they have developed their own style of hospitality that allows them to reach excellence, and create a memorable customer experience.

The truth is, most organizations within the hospitality industry strive to achieve excellence, and only a select few are actually able to do so. Some continuously measure their quality of service through metrics and "mystery guests" to gauge how effective associates are at following protocol, standards, and procedures established by the brand. They're looking for a real-time glimpse into how customers experience their brand, and whether those customers come back again.

Organizations waste huge amounts of money conducting this type of research, hiring agencies to assess and report the quality of service. The real data is gathered directly from the customer. How do you handle feedback from someone who visited two, three, maybe even four weeks ago? Do you call that guest directly? One hardly even considers that option. Do send an email apology if a guest complains? Yes, though most likely with a generic prototype that has been sent repeatedly after prior visits, and prior complaints.

Wouldn't it be more beneficial to recover the guest experience before they depart?

And wouldn't the opportunity for immediate feedback then grant you the opportunity for an immediate reaction in order to recover that guest experience?

What could happen if you responded not only to complaints, but also to glowing reviews from satisfied customers, with a personalized letter rather than a prototype?

At Changi Airport, they measure visitor feedback at the same moment those visitors receive the service. They provide visitor feedback kiosks at every touchpoint. Service recovery happens in that same instant. These measurements are functional: excellent, good, average, poor, or very poor. This system is simple to understand, utilizing images rather than asking visitors to read a lot of text or have to choose a preferred language. It's authentic because they do something about it. They don't just collect metrics and let them sit unused; they react immediately to recover the guest experience. And they monitor, in order to avoid a repeat situation.

Many companies and airports use similar systems in an effort to address customer concerns. The key difference at Changi Airport is that a resolution occurs in the moment, as soon as a customer selects poor or average service from the feedback options, that data is transferred to a customer service agent, who is then able to recover the customer experience in an instant. Too often we enter a run-of-the-mill restaurant, store, or hotel, and complaints are treated as an inconvenience to the staff (rather than the customer). You're told that nothing can be done, or that such and such goes against their policies or some other excuse.

You can always do something to address the complaint. Make sure it's functional, keep it simple, and be authentic, and go the extra step to look for a solution.

I was once giving a workshop on leadership for hotel managers in Madrid. I asked a question that everyone in my audience struggled to answer. I asked them to define their hospitality style.

One person said, "I am empathetic." Another said, "I make things happen immediately." Answers varied, including statements about being customer-oriented, a good listener, passionate, always looking for quality over quantity, being excellent at resolving situations and complaints, being good strategically, and so on.

Those answers are all good, but they don't define your style. Your style is not about personal strength. It's about how you use those strengths to create the style you want to implement in your entire organization.

Your customer experience delivery is dependent on your hospitality style. Remember, your hospitality style is defined by who you are, what you offer, what you believe, and your principles. It's your values, your people, your leadership, and your management.

Finding your hospitality style means identifying your principles, as I shared for the three company examples earlier. Those principles will help you define the style you would like to adopt, making you the master of your customers' experience.

Questions

- Share this chapter with your team. Answer the following questions and then have your leaders/managers answer them.
- Define your hospitality style.
- What are your organization's service values and how do you make them stylish?
- How do you prepare your associates to adopt your hospitality style with the goal of becoming better than best?

Actions to Take

To master your style or the style you already have I recommend you to implement at your organization the ten steps that make you stylish.

Look into details that can make the difference. For example, each time I go to Citibank for a transaction they send me the same email signed by the person who delivered the service.

The content is the following:

> This is just a reminder of how important it is for us to have you as a client.
>
> Thank you for visiting Citibank @ ....
>
> It was a pleasure assisting you today!
>
> My personal goal is to ensure that I have processed your transaction in an accurate and timely manner while meeting your expectations.
>
> We appreciate your business.

> Thank you for being a loyal client of Citibank signing by the name of the person who gave me the service.

This is a nice email from Citibank, but they are not making the difference. It is the same email they send to every single customer. Nothing special. It becomes a bunch of deleted emails.

But what if, instead of sending an email each time I visit, the manager sent me a personal email where he mentioned that I visited his bank four times this month and that next time I am at the bank to please ask for them to meet me in person and thank me personally for being a loyal client? That is how you make the difference.

Here are some other examples:

- **Listening.** To exceed the expectations of your customer, it is a must to listen and observe your customer style and behavior.
- **Visioning.** Create a broad view of what's possible for you. Once you have a vision about how you want to deliver your service. Creativity takes part in making that vision a reality.
- **Innovating.** Innovation is the fuel of your business. I always say innovation is your maintenance doctor. You have to do a check-up every year to see how healthy you are. It is exactly the same. Each year, check how your business is positioned in the market and whether it is becoming dated and needs some fresh and innovative ideas.
- **Learning is about approaching your internal customers —your associates—with the help they need to improve.** To improve your service, you need to:
- **Trust:** Do I trust you to work for you? To work with you? To buy from you? To be loyal to your brand? Those are questions subconsciously your internal customers,

external customers, and vendors are asking themselves. The authenticity of your story, whether on a personal or professional level, is the column that builds trust.

- **Be present and proactive.** Be present with your customers on what you hear, what you see, what you feel, and what you ask. Be proactive to help them understand your vision, exceed their expectations, and fascinate and amaze them with your unexpected details.
- **Adapt.** Do internal customers feel they are treated as you ask them to treat your customers or your guests? By understanding their needs, circumstances, and challenges your internal customers are facing, you can adapt your recruitment and internal training to those needs. It makes internal customers embrace the concept of delivering the experience you are seeking.
- **Be prepared.** By preparing your internal customers you move them to experimenting and delivering better experience. Having more experience or being promoted in your job doesn't mean you are more knowledgeable. You build knowledge when you are prepared.
- **Model leaders.** By modeling leaders you are able to cultivate a customer experience culture so contagious that internal customers can't help but master it, live it, and transmit it to others every day.
- **Understand** the significance of each of the above improvements.
- **Consider every service, product, and presentation.** You will be surprised how many goals you will be able to achieve because of these elements.
- **Blend your principles, service values, key service into your style by using the three secret elements: functionality, simplicity, and authenticity**. It is not about changing your standard; it is about taking your service to the next level.

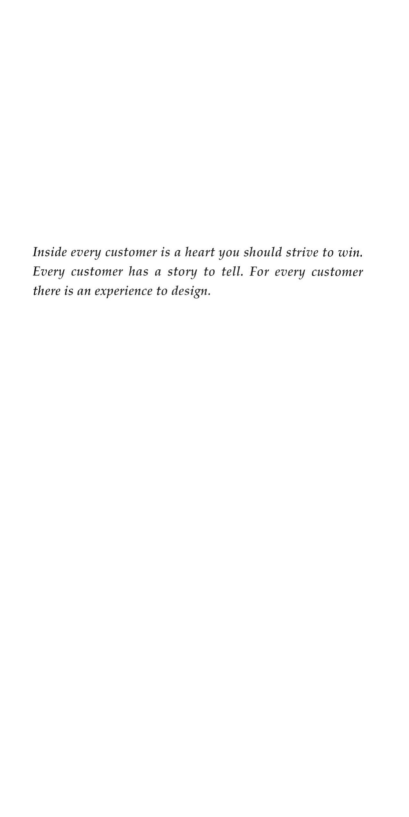

Inside every customer is a heart you should strive to win. Every customer has a story to tell. For every customer there is an experience to design.

2

Your Associates Are the Heartbeat of Your Organization

I t is imperative that the culture established either directly by you, or by your organization, comes from the heart. This loving philosophy must then translate easily to both customers and associates.

However, unfortunately what I have found over years of working with many different organizations is that the company culture is unclear. Their internal customers—the associates—are unable to understand and take ownership of the company values. Often organizations attempt to solve for this disconnect by hiring outside consultants, who come in and conduct a market study focused on the external customer. What ends up happening is that the essence of the company, the estate, and the internal customers' opinions, beliefs, and values are neglected.

And this undermines any effort made to create a cohesive, effective culture that is easy to understand and easily applied at all levels of the organization.

In this chapter, you will learn how to address culture issues for good through what I call the heartbeat: your associates, your customers, your culture, and your service.

Heartbeat Your Associates

In 2006, I was hired by a company in Cancún, Mexico, to enhance standard and procedure protocols, as well as design and implement a new brand culture. We were working on something entirely new for the company: a lifestyle concept that was unfamiliar to all members of the organization. Our challenge was to ensure that everyone involved not only understood the meaning of customer experience, but also bought into and believed the new culture wholeheartedly since this particular property was to act as the pilot for the global brand.

It was crucial for me to have the total support of the leaders and managers by the time I was developing and implementing the customer experience concept of the new brand.

I was charged with transforming a three-star, all-inclusive hotel in a luxury lifestyle hotel under the European Plan.

At the time of this project, very few people understood the meaning of customer experience, nor were they familiar with the concept of a lifestyle hotel.

My primary objective was to design a customer experience strategy that would prove to be more powerful than the competition, and unique in the marketplace. For my own market research, I decided to travel to Miami and Las Vegas to study the best luxury lifestyle hotels in the industry and see what we could do to differentiate our own brand.

Back in Cancún, my first challenge was to ensure that everyone within the organization truly understood both the meaning of customer experience and the idea behind the new brand.

Let me demonstrate what I mean.

My title on my business card is Experience Director. Each time I give my card to someone new, the initial reaction is one of confusion when they read this title. And joking.

"Um, experience director? What kind of experience can you do for me?"

I would answer, "Um, that depends!"

This response is always followed by laughter.

But really, there are so many ways to answer the above question. It could take all day to explore all the nuances of what I do, and explain the steps and strategies to enhance customer experience.

The best explanation I have of what experience directors do is that we are ambassadors of the brand. It is our mission to create memorable experiences for both our internal and external customers, so that we are in turn creating ambassadors out of them as well.

That principle is easy to state, but often difficult for people around you to believe and embrace. This is especially true when it comes to dealing with associates and managers with a fixed mindset, fixed habits, and no desire for change.

For the Cancún project, I was facing multiple barriers from general managers who were unwilling to buy into the concept and support the idea.

Often, after a presentation on any project within the new customer experience concept and strategy, the reaction I would get was what I refer to as the No-No Effect.

Later in this book I will teach you how to handle No-Nos, but first, let me explain what I mean by this.

How many times have you had someone on your team show up with a negative attitude, or destroy anyone else's ideas for the sole purpose of asserting their own point of view, or trying to downplay that your opinion is not good enough?

You get the sense that this behavior stems from the fact that whatever idea is in question isn't their own. So they dig their heels in and make things difficult.

The No-Nos are always looking for small things that can destroy an idea. And one of the most important and effective ways to enhance internal and external customer experience is by using positive communication.

No-Nos are not welcome in the customer experience world.

When we create or deliver actions designed to enhance customer experience, we are going outside the status quo, sometimes by breaking or bypassing the rules. There are many managers and leaders who do not handle this well.

For example, we may decide that instead of having the check-in for oceanfront rooms at the main reception in the lobby, we want to handle it in-room. We want to change procedures in order to wow the customer, and provide more value for their selected room category. At the same time, we are able to familiarize the customer with the in-room facilities, and take advantage of any opportunities to cross-sell other services or amenities.

Some managers may be irritated by this change to their set routine and logistics. But, we would argue, the sense of arrival for the customer has been greatly enhanced from the usual standard.

It's not always easy to sell everyone within an organization on the value behind a customer experience concept.

I remember my presentation to an executive team in the Dominican Republic. The general manager listened to what I had to say, and responded with an objection.

"Very nice presentation, Johnny. But we do not sell experiences here, we sell beds. You're asking me to break up the staffing guide, with an executive on board, and I don't see the revenue behind this move. When guest experience can bring in more revenue than beds, then I'd be happy to accept your offer."

It is not easy to get leaders to buy into your concept. And if the leaders aren't on board, the associates' belief in the concept and new brand culture will be even lower.

It's not enough to introduce the customer experience concept and new culture, and try out the new ways of operating. It is imperative to stick to the new practices, and new ways of behaving, until everyone is confident in their success and they replace the old traditions.

I could try to make the internal customer understand and believe in the new culture, but how could I make it stick long enough to become the day-to-day level of performance?

How could I make these service values become part of the behavior of each associate?

How could I ensure everyone within the company sees a customer experience opportunity at every touchpoint and customer interaction?

My biggest challenge in Cancún was showing everyone within that company that the change would be real, and worth the initial upheaval.

To do this, I had to start with the top leaders. I needed them to understand, accept the new culture, embrace changes, support it, and follow the vision and strategy that we would design together.

I decided to start with the essential, most impactful actions.

Within the human resources department, we launched a campaign asking for volunteers to become culture advisors. We ended up securing around 50 volunteers in total. Then, every three weeks, one leader from each department would be assigned to lead a different group of advisors, who had a different mission to support the implementation of the new culture.

The communication between leaders and advisors proved to be highly effective.

By adding the support of those advisors to the launch of the new culture, we were able to replace old traditions with new behaviors in a short period of time, and succeed.

But I needed to address gaps in team interactions between the different departments.

I recognized that it was time to go aggressively outside the box and do something that would be contagious. It also had to be easy to remember, and easy to implement.

In came the idea for the heart greeting. The heart greeting is a traditional way of greeting people in Lebanon, my home country. In Lebanon, this gesture is made between friends and people whom you appreciate. The Lebanese are expressive people; we use body language, facial expressions, and gestures for much of our communication.

The heart greeting I had in mind to implement is a gesture in which you place the open palm of your right hand over your heart when you greet someone. It can easily be used for every person you cross paths with—internal customers, external customers, vendors, partners, visitors—no matter which position you hold.

Greeting everyone was part of the new culture we were implementing, as a show of respect between colleagues as well as visitors. But when I first presented this idea to the brand's vice president, I was met with a No-No reaction. He did grant his approval to try it, even though he wasn't convinced of its effectiveness, or what it had to do with the customer experience and revenue.

I decided to take the risk, and started testing the greeting with the internal customers. I acted as an example, and implemented this heart greeting with everyone I came into contact with. This was a break from tradition when it came to the rules of a luxury lifestyle hotel, but it caught on. Eventually, all of us within the organization were using the greeting, both while on property and even when crossing paths outside the work environment. It became a source of pride, an unspoken symbol of mutual regard and respect.

This gesture became a strong indicator of how much we had evolved from the old brand. We were able to use the simple action of placing an open palm over the heart as a tool to embrace the new branding, without anything complicated to understand or memorize. It became a real heartbeat.

And it started one habit at a time.

Tackling change one habit at a time helps ensure that everyone involved is following the new action, and believing in the direction you are moving and what is needed to achieve success. Culture cannot be built in a single day. A new habit, however, can be adopted in a much shorter amount of time than it takes to shift an entire brand. With persistence, that habit can spread throughout the entire organization until it becomes the norm.

With the heart greeting, we were able to cultivate a work environment in which employees felt involved and invested in the new brand. That was the key to our success.

But the goal of the greeting wasn't only about colleagues and employees; it involved external customers as well. Customers became curious about the gesture, and the associates were proud to explain its meaning as well as the story behind it.

Surprisingly, we started receiving positive feedback that our associates were connecting emotionally with customers by greeting them from their heart; this simple gesture was becoming known, and external customers were responding with the same greeting, showing just how effectively this new customer experience habit was starting to soak into the fabric of the brand.

Though it took a full six months for it to be fully adopted, this greeting became an effective way to promote our brand at events, and to show our customers exactly how we stand apart from the competition. The heart greeting was the starting point of the new customer experience journey.

It's through ideas such as this that you'll be able to heartbeat your employees.

Heartbeat Your Customer

In 2012, I went on a twenty-five-day holiday in Thailand with my wife. For the first seven days, we stayed at the Banyan Tree Bangkok. I had two days of work before I could officially be out of the office, which I spent giving workshops to a French group on enhancing customer experience and leadership training.

Early on the third morning, I approached the reception staff of our hotel and informed them that in four days' time I would be spending a week's holiday with my wife at the Banyan Tree Samui, on the island of Koh Samui, and I wanted to organize transportation from the airport to the hotel.

"Yes, Mr. Sfeir, we will arrange transport for you."

Upon our arrival on Koh Samui, we found a gentleman waiting for us at the airport holding a sign with our names and a welcome letter. That is expected when you request a driver, and our check-in at the hotel was smooth, as it should be in a five-star hotel.

What was unexpected was the amenity waiting for us at our villa.

During our stay in Bangkok, I developed a taste for these honey peanuts that were sold by an old man across the street from the hotel. I ate these homemade peanuts every day we were in the city. The housekeeper once asked me about one of the peanut bags I had in the room. She spoke only Thai, and I do not, but we were able to communicate well enough through gestures and body language for me to tell her that I bought them from the man across the street. She smiled, pleased that I was enjoying the local street vendors.

Unbeknownst to me, this housekeeper had shared my penchant for these peanuts with the customer service staff of the hotel, who then sent the hotel on Koh Samui two bags of the peanuts, with a picture of the man, Kasem, and a note saying he hopes to see me back again soon.

This was the amenity we discovered upon arrival. It was a true heartbeat moment.

Heartbeat moments occurred throughout our stay at Koh Samui. Our first morning, the villa security guard, who already knew me by name, greeted me as I was heading out for an early run. When I returned, a basket was waiting for me, containing an energy bar, a wet towel, a bottle of water, and a map of routes to run in the area for my next outing.

The next morning at breakfast, after filling my plate from the sumptuous buffet, I found a French newspaper waiting for me at our table. It was accompanied by a note that read, "We are aware you were giving a conference in Bangkok for a group of French, and though we know you are not French, we thought you may enjoy reading this." At my wife's place was a Spanish newspaper—they knew she was from Spain.

This hotel knew exactly how to craft an unforgettable experience, both during our stay and afterward. For instance, we still receive notes from the general manager on our birthdays each year, even though it's been many years since we visited. And these emotional moments have lasting positive effects.

In the world of hospitality, you should give excellent service. But not everyone knows how to deliver memorable experiences. And it's through such skill that you create ambassadors for your brand.

I promote Banyan Tree Samui every chance I get—in every talk, in every training, and now here in the pages of this book.

Some of the people might be put off by the level of personal knowledge companies have access to. However, it's not a question of knowing every single thing in your life, but rather an attention to the specific details that can surprise and delight a guest. These are the key to creating memories out of moments and securing a fan for life.

Your mission as a customer experience designer is to find a way for your brand culture to transition from your associates' heads to their hearts. Only then can they deliver a level of service that touches the heart of the customer.

At the Banyan Tree properties in Thailand, you can feel that they operate from their own hearts, and you can see the difference that it makes.

Heartbeat Your Culture

Culture is paramount to a company's success, and maintaining your culture does not happen on its own. The stories above demonstrate two compelling examples of culture and customer experience.

It is your culture that helps you design your customer experience as the design of your customer experience helps you to sustain your culture.

If your culture is neglected and absent from the day-to-day behavior of your leaders and associates, it's nothing more than a bunch of toilet paper, if you'll forgive my expression.

As I've mentioned previously, implementing and then maintaining a culture and customer experience is not an easy job. And it is not just the responsibility of the human resources department. It rests on the shoulders of every person within your organization to bring the culture to life, and to seek out the details that will make your customer experience not just acceptable, but excellent.

Culture begins on Day One for anyone associated with your brand. Orientation for new hires typically begins with introductions to the company mission, vision, and values. Perhaps there are a few posters on the walls, or brochures, or a playbook filled with reminders for employees. This is a great starting point, but the process actually begins before the orientation—before you've even made the hire.

You want to select people for your team with the brand culture in mind. You want to find people who love your brand or love the idea of working for you. We will go over this in more detail in a later chapter, but this is an essential component for creating and maintaining your culture.

Most organizations don't understand why they have a high level of turnover. They blame the geographic location, market demand, culture of the country, managers for poor leadership, human resources for poor recruitment—the list goes on.

In reality, the culprit is the culture. A great culture is what every organization needs to create a great internal and external customer experience. If your associates love the culture, and they feel it, live it, and reinforce it daily, then you have been able to achieve a positive environment and happy internal customers. Happy associates are the beginning of a positive customer experience journey, which leads to sustainable success. It is through a strong culture and an internal customer experience strategy that you will be able to gain the loyalty of your associates

Your associates are the beating heart of your organization.

Regardless of how absorbed we become by technology or dominated by online sales, people who demonstrate true service through the heart can never be substituted when it comes to building relationships and loyalty.

In my years in the hospitality industry, I have worked with many leaders who still believe that creating an intentional culture is a waste of time and money. They do not understand the value of culture, the meaning behind it, and how powerful it can be in leading your organization toward success. And this becomes a problem for their brands.Culture is a collection of behaviors and shared values that help support your entire organization in acting, reacting, and behaving at the same high level. Culture is the reputation of your brand. It is the key to your success, in both internal and external customer experience. As management guru Peter Drucker is credited with saying, "Culture eats strategy for breakfast."

Bright leaders understand the importance of culture, and the power to follow-through. Strong company culture can only be crafted if managers believe in it, and deliver on it every single day.

Powerful culture produces happy associates, which creates excellent customer experience, which builds sustainable success.

Questions

Are you willing to take your service to the next level and enhance your internal and external customer experience? How are you willing to do it? List four ideas.

Do you have a meaningful and loving culture? List three service values or three aspects of your culture that are loved by your internal customers as well as your external customers.

Are your service values or service behaviors easy to remember? If yes, mention an example. If not, how can you make them easy to remember? The more ideas you have, the better the results.

Do you have a contagious or a virus element at your organization? Describe them.

What is your strategy to keep your culture alive? List at least eight strategies.

Have you ever asked your internal customers about their beliefs and values? If yes, how did you do it? If not, how will you do it?

Actions to Take

- Make sure your service values match with your brand and are easy to understand and apply. If they do, the match is fantastic. If not, start solving the puzzle.
- Make sure your managers and leaders are transmitting your culture on a daily basis. Ask them to come up with a plan where you share your culture every day with your team and others.
- Ask for volunteers to help you increase your ambassador directory.
- Make sure managers/leaders are working hand in hand with human resources to apply new, positive behaviors.
- Make sure that managers/leaders use a plan that it is fun, exciting, and enjoyable to remember and share.
- Ask your internal customers about the culture and make sure they love and believe in your organization's values. If you think that your culture needs adjustment, do it. Your employee turnover will go down.

Growth is less about the concept and more about the people behind it. Hire the right people to build your customers experiences from roots to fruits.

3

Handle the No-Nos

The No-Nos are enemies of your customer experience. It's always apparent on your team who is the No-No and who is the Yes-Yes.

A No-No will always react to any idea brought to the table with *but, maybe,* or *no.*

Here are other ways you'll recognize a No-No:

- A No-No is driven by a bad attitude.
- A No-No looks for the negative in any situation or idea.
- A No-No is the destroyer of any idea or concept.
- A No-No believes only their idea is good.
- A No-No always looks for mistakes made by others.
- A No-No focuses on the past.
- A No-No blames others.
- A No-No uses the phrase, "I told you so. Nobody listened."
- A No-No always wants to win.

A No-No will send you an email—copying everyone in the office —with a complaint, or questioning why X, Y, or Z is the way it is. This is typical behavior for people caught up in a No-No perspective, attempting to make sure they are heard, and trying to show everyone that they are committed to the job and on top of everything that is happening within the company or department. Nonsense. What's really happening is that they've put on their "Superman cape," and are unable to realize it.

But be aware, the No-No persona exists within all of us. You are not exempt from falling into the trap of negatively focused thinking and behaviors. Let's say you have a list of pending items on your to-do list, and you decide to put them off another day, then another day, and onwards. This is you saying no to the tasks at hand, instead of saying yes, these are all doable.

Whereas No-Nos hinder your efforts, a positive attitude and leadership style provide the foundation for customer experience. You cannot enhance your customer experience through negativity; this is not the way to become a skilled leader for a bright future. Customer experience requires a leader with an open mindset, one who is ready to listen to new ideas, and who is willing to support and test those new ideas.

There are three areas that could potentially disrupt your leadership:

- Managing No-Nos in meetings
- Managing No-Nos as a leader
- Managing your own No-No

It is imperative to your success that you learn the strategies for how to handle these.

Managing No-Nos in Meetings

A meeting is a crucial opportunity to improve communication and achieve goals. I used to cringe during meetings when a general manager asked each person around the table to take a turn to speak. What would usually end up happening is that each person would talk about his or her own issues and needs, and the "blame game" would commence.

I'll use a typical hotel meeting as an example. Let's say it's the reception manager's turn to speak, and they share that a VIP guest complained about an air conditioning issue, and ask that maintenance step in to help reach a resolution. This manager also has another guest who requested compensation because the food on the buffet wasn't deemed to be five-star quality.

The maintenance manager acts as No-No by responding that the customer must not know how to use the air conditioning system in the first place. Maybe all the AC controllers in all five hundred rooms should be changed.

The chef acts as a No-No by defending the buffet, saying that the customer must not have any idea of the quality of the products on offer. The chef puts the blame on the customer's perceived lack of knowledge, as well as a recent 30 percent budget cut that doesn't leave room for purchasing higher quality. This response is rife with buts.

The general manager questions the ability to finance this feedback, and the managers of the other departments are all sitting there listening, and criticizing. The meeting has swiftly turned to chaos, with no one on the same page about anything. Each person is thinking about themselves, and their department, and doesn't care to consider the others.

The No-Nos started with the reception manager and the customer complaints that pointed toward lousy functioning by other departments. That approach provokes defensive answers and is not productive in a meeting. Solutions can be sought without dragging everyone into it.

Meetings should not be held to present customers complaints or problems or ask for favors. Instead, meetings should be a place to:

- Achieve goals and set new challenges.
- Motivate and build camaraderie.
- Create a plan of action.
- Surprise and engage your team.
- Build enthusiasm.
- Present where you are, and where you want to be.
- Remind everyone what you stand for.
- Increase creativity and incomes.
- Design new strategies.
- Impact others emotionally.
- Enhance your internal and external customer experience.
- Have fun, learn something new, be encouraged, and build excitement for the next meeting.

A leader has to know how to both manage meetings and eliminate the No-Nos at the table.

The framework I outline below will help you manage your meetings successfully and create a superior customer experience without leaving room for No-Nos to interfere or sabotage the meeting.

But First, No Excuses Accepted

Excuses arise in meetings when someone is late, or they arrive unprepared. You can prevent lateness by creating something silly to "punish" anyone who isn't punctual. This "punishment" must be fun—you're not trying to disrespect anyone—but nobody should really want to do it. You want to coach a new behavior and discipline, not create resentment. I have used this approach many times with great success.

Here's an example of how it could work. Let's say you create a rule that the first time someone is late to a meeting, that person will be handed a yellow card as a penalty, like in soccer. The second time, a red card is given. The third time, that person is responsible for providing and serving breakfast to everyone in the room.

The caveat is that the breakfast must be personalized, and can be served either during the meeting, at an attendee's office, or at an attendee's convenience. This third "punishment" could take quite a bit more time, depending on how many meeting attendees there are, providing a harmless but powerful motivation for showing up on time. But, to give a little leeway, team members are allowed to be late—but only for a total of six minutes per month. And everyone must commit to this.

The no-excuses rule combined with the framework below will ensure that your meetings run smoothly. This framework must be completed on paper two days prior to the meeting date, without fail.

The five points of the framework are:

- **Declare your want.** State your intentions, and what you want from the meeting.
- I**dentify your potential idea and give a 360-degree view of it.** Develop an idea, and then brainstorm from as many angles as you can to create a plan of action, who will be responsible, and a timeframe for achievement.
- **Plan for priorities to resolve.** Conceptualize potential complications before they happen and become an emergency, and create alternate plans to address each scenario.
- **Consider the emotional impact.** Describe the emotional impact you plan to create—the why behind the idea—for both the internal and external customer.

- **Agree to the rule of No-Nos.** Commit to showing up with a positive attitude and being open to hearing other ideas and plans of action. No judgments, no criticisms.

Every attendee is given a full fifteen minutes to speak, and then the "microphone" is passed to the next person.

I used to use silence for the rest of the meeting as a penalty if someone judged or criticized any of the suggestions or ideas presented, or for any negative comment.

Imagine how much more could be accomplished if each person showed up to each meeting having agreed to the rules, and with this framework completed.

Managing No-Nos as a Leader

No-No attitudes within your team will be one of your greatest obstacles to overcome as a leader.

On many occasions, a team member will not recognize their own negative energy or even be aware of the habits that contribute to an undesired outcome.

No-Nos tend to automatically react to suggestions with statements such as "This isn't going to work" or "We tried this already, without results." These comments are both negative and unhelpful. But the person saying them rarely identifies as negative, or unhelpful. Often they're packaged as being realistic.

This is a classic example of a No-No.

Why does this happen?

It boils down to an inclination to win. A No-No wants to show everyone at the table that they are in control. In reality, none of it is true. People do not want a leader who wants to win at any cost and shows off how smart they perceive themselves to be. This is not a leader who inspires for the future.

As a leader, you don't need to prove that you are worthy of your position. You have already earned it, and now your primary responsibility is to show up as the capable leader your company needs.

Managing Your Own No-Nos

Do you often react negatively? Could you perhaps be a No-No? Maybe you are, and maybe you're not. You may react negatively because:

- You're impulsive.
- You're stressed.
- You're in a rush and other people are slowing you down or "stealing" your time.
- You're in a bad mood.
- You're under pressure.
- You reject the opinions of those you don't like.
- You think differently.
- You don't trust someone.
- You're stuck with certain procedures and see no way out.

None of the above determines who you are as a person. Most likely, you question yourself when you react in a negative way. If you don't, you should start now. Awareness is the first step to managing your own No-No. Knowing how you behave in certain situations will support you in learning how to overcome any tendencies that don't serve you as a leader.

A No-No attitude won't help in your relationships within your team, your peers, your customers, yourself, or even your personal life. When you are always on the lookout for something that's wrong with an idea or comment, you come across as insecure. It demonstrates your lack of trust in your team, and in yourself.

I am considered to be a positive person in all aspects. But believe me, I put in the effort to increase my awareness, and address my own negative reactions in order to become the positive person I am today. First, I had to stop identifying as a victim whenever someone said something I don't agree with. I had to start accepting that I'm not always right, and I can at times be wrong. Managing my thoughts remains a full-time job, one that I recommit to on a daily basis.

Remember that negative thoughts stem from a fear of failure.

I realize that there are many leaders who aren't thrilled about the prospect of not being right. Those leaders are scared of screwing up, afraid of failing.

Transforming No-No thoughts into Yes-Yes thoughts requires being aware of your own bullshit, and replacing it with the positive, and demonstrating trust in yourself and your people.

Trust plays a significant part for a customer experience designer. The ability to trust your people shows that you trust yourself. You need to be able to trust that your people will do their best to delight your customers, and support you in achieving your goals.

Too often we stick to the motto that people have to show us they're trustworthy in order for us to trust them. You could try to go about it this way, but who is the one trusting first? You, or your associate? It goes both ways. As the leader, it is your responsibility to create the opportunity for trust to flourish. It's on you to go first.

If someone messes up, that's okay. There's no need to cast blame. Convert the mess up into a Yes-Yes opportunity, and handle the situation in a positive manner.

Trust is the key element in enhancing customer experience. You must show trust by being someone known for a Yes-Yes attitude, not as a No-No.

Operating from a place of Yes-Yes encourages those around you to adopt the Yes-Yes mentality. In that sort of environment, and No-Nos will be squeezed out, deprived of the negativity on which they thrive.

But it's not about just saying yes to anything and everything. It's about maintaining positivity and receptivity to ideas, information, and comments. It's about presenting your thoughts with confidence, and the manner in which you interact with others. It's about forging an identity as a positive person who is capable of spreading that high vibration energy within your sphere of influence, associates, and customers alike.

Positive people tend to be the happiest people, and your customers will sense this. You want to be surrounded by happy people, and so do they.

Positivity for a customer experience designer is looking toward what has been defined as impossible in the minds of others and finding a way to make it possible.

Positivity is how you focus your own mind, and the minds of your customers, to a joyful moment.

Positivity is the transformation of No-No's from the blind, dark world of denying what's possible into the brightness of unlimited possibility.

Positivity will make you a stronger leader, not a weaker one.

Commit to being more positive, starting now.

Questions and Actions

What are your first signs of recognition that you're dealing with a No-No, whether in someone else, or in yourself? What steps will you take immediately to turn that negativity around?

Write down two or three instances where you successfully reversed a No-No attitude, and make note of any "surefire strategy" you feel you can use in virtually any situation. Then create a plan to share it with your team leaders. Role playing in team meetings might be a great way to get the point across about how important it is to nip negativity in the bud.

Don't stop with your own ideas. Create a survey asking your employees how they turn negative attitudes around. Read the better responses aloud or do a PowerPoint in your next team meeting, and have the team vote on the three methods they feel are most effective. Use this to create consensus among team members so that consistency is taught, practiced, and retained.

Excellent service starts with passion. Achievements start with a vision. Expert delivery starts within you.

4

Hire and Prepare Your Team

No matter your business model, inviting the right people to join your team and preparing them to thrive is the backbone of your customer experience strategy.

You can have the best product in the world, the best service culture, the best philosophy, but without the right leaders in place and associates who are able to execute correctly, your customer experience strategy will fail.

When we like a product or brand, it's difficult to get us to change loyalties. We become attached to the quality of service, the facilities, or the people, and switching to another company feels risky.

For example, consider your home internet service. If your service provider is doing a fantastic job—excellent service, delivering what you pay for, 24/7 support—the chances of you changing to a different provider is quite low.

The only way to change a customer's mind about using a new company is to:

- Find values that the current company is not offering.

- Make those values clear through new offers and outstanding service.
- Evaluate these offers based on what makes them unique.
- Provide similar or better pricing that reflects the values that attract the customer away from the current company.

If these factors aren't considered, the chances of effectively influencing a customer's decision to use a different service are minimal.

Winning in customer experience requires you to surround yourself with the right people to support your mission and attract new customers.

Hiring effectively is a skill, one that I have been honing since the beginning of my professional career. And if there's one thing I've learned, it's that your hiring strategy, recruiting, and preparation of your team must evolve as your brand and markets grow.

My Own Journey Getting Hired

In 1990, I applied for a sales director position at the Librería General in Zaragoza, Spain. Now, this was a while ago. You might be thinking that things have changed since the turn of the millennium. But believe me, it's not all that different between then and now.

We still rely on the same templates of questionnaires and psychology tests, only today's younger generations have become quite savvy at working the system when filling these out. They know how to take tests and score well, and prepare for interviews with the help of coaches, online courses, and professional mentors. But resources were fewer back in the mid-1990s.

This interview at the library in Spain would have been my first job in management. I wasn't experienced enough for the position, and in my mind, I'd already decided that I wasn't going to get it. I wasn't even nervous about this fact. I'd been told no before. I was more curious about how I would handle being in an interview for a next-level position. It was an exercise in discovery for me, meant to help me better understand the interview process.

I first learned of the position from a headhunter and consultant. Those guys were the experts in recruiting executives for large companies. I was told that this library was looking for a sales director and had already interviewed thirty people. I was the last one on the list. The process would start with an oral interview, and if I passed that, I would need to fill out an assessment that would take up to five hours to complete. After that was done, they would call me within the following three days, or not.

There were no mobile phones back in those days. When you were awaiting news, you had to sit by the phone. Or near the door in case a telegram arrived. This could potentially be quite a lengthy process.

The oral interview began with a typical question from the hiring manager.

"Why did you apply for the job?"

"In your ad, you mentioned to only apply if you think you're the best. That's why I applied for this position because I believe I'm your best option," I replied.

"You sound quite confident about that. Why do you believe I should interview you?"

"I'm glad you asked that question. I realize I have no background as a sales director, but I was born selling diapers to my mom. Selling is something that comes naturally to me, and that I enjoy. At my last job, I was able to outsell all of the other sales agents and increase revenue more in three months than they had done for the company in eight years. Is that a good reason for you to interview me?"

"I believe so."

Then he asked me a less conventional question.

"How would your best friends describe you?"

That one was less easy to answer, but I didn't let it intimidate me.

"They'd say I'm a fun, crazy, enthusiastic, creative, sexy, loving person who is ambitious and elegant, and loyal above all else."

Then he asked if I would rate myself on a scale of one to ten in certain areas.

He started with confidence. "I will rate for you: ten," he laughed.

"Thank you," I answered, "I believe I am a seven."

"Why so?"

"I believe that ten is perfection, seven to eight is ideal, nine is insecure."

He laughed and said, "You are right."

For presentation skills, I rated myself an eight.

"Why an eight?" he asked

"I enjoy talking in public and observing people's reactions. I love asking questions and interacting. I love the adrenaline that comes with being on stage."

The last one he asked was about accepting rejection.

I rated myself a two.

"I can see that you hate rejection."

"I always try not to give any reasons to reject me. Now is a perfect example."

He laughed.

"Johnny, if you are rejected, I imagine that you get upset?"

"I'd get upset with myself. But that's not the case here."

The banter continued for the duration of the hourlong interview.

In the end, the hiring manager shared that I did well enough to continue on to the written portion of the interview process. I braced myself for the challenge. I had five hours to complete the assessment, and it was already midday. I'd have to read fast, avoid distractions, and not waste time in order to be done by 5:00 p.m.

The assessment was a multiple-choice format. It should have been simple enough, except I tend to get nervous during written exams. I lose focus and lose time re-reading every question and second-guessing my answers. In addition, this assessment was in Spanish, and it was safe to say that my written language skills weren't quite up to snuff at that time. In short, I was dreading this next step.

I found myself moving at a snail's pace for the first hour of the exam. I would never be able to pass this exam at this rate. I had a choice to either give in to my nerves, which were screaming at me that I would never pass, I was certain to fail, and so on, or I could square up and change tactics.

I made the choice to be more decisive and committed to reading the remaining questions once and give my best answer. No wavering. Ninety minutes later, I was finished. I wasn't confident I'd aced it, but I found freedom in the release of all expectations.

When the consulting agency called me the next day, I was convinced they would tell me I was out of the running for the position. Instead, they invited me to their office. I wasn't sure what to expect—possibly another dreaded written assessment—so I turned up in jeans and a T-shirt. To my surprise, upon entering the meeting room, I was standing face to face not only with the consultant who headhunted me, but with two advisors and the president of the Librería General as well.

I heard them say I got the job at the same time as I heard the pop of a champagne bottle. I had been selected from a pool of thirty applicants, each top-rated in their field. I thought to myself surely this must be some sort of joke.

"Is this a joke?" I asked, a smile on my face, "Because if it is, it's a bad one."

They started laughing. The champagne was already flowing, so I decided to celebrate along with them. They believed I was joking, and I was still looking for signs to call their bluff. I played the winning hand though, and went along with this strange charade, talking about anything and everything except work.

At one point the CEO turned serious, and said, "Johnny, I am expecting a huge achievement from you. I'm counting on you to open the international market and make Librería General the number one export in Spain, and increase our sales to two hundred million pesetas."

"I will make this happen, sir. With this champagne, I can make anything you ask a reality. Is there more champagne, by the way?"

The room laughed, as did I. But I noted a more serious undertone to this exchange.

The euro was yet to become the common currency of Europe. Two hundred million pesetas at that time was the equivalent of

$1.3 million today. This was a daunting task. I left the meeting even more convinced that they had to be bluffing in hiring me.

I called the human resources department, fully expecting they would confirm my suspicion that the position did indeed go to someone more qualified. I was told that yes, the job was mine, and they were very much looking forward to meeting me on Monday morning. I froze, unsure of how to reply. When my brain came back to earth, the realization that I had just landed this highly coveted job hit me—immediately followed by the second realization that I was in over my head.

Still hesitant, I showed up at the corporate office that Monday morning, pen and paper in hand, a smile on my face. I was given the grand tour and was presented to the entire corporate team. I was shown the massive office that would be mine, along with a generous salary. I even had my own sales team, who would report directly to me. And I had absolutely no idea what to do with any of it, or where to even start.

I knew that my assigned mission was to increase revenue and introduce the Spanish book market to the larger international market. But I felt entirely alone in this, like I had no support in figuring out how to accomplish this. No one in the organization really understood my position; they didn't know my job description, and couldn't help me figure out my first step. I had to learn by asking the team. I needed their ideas to help me get going, and deciding what to do.

This created tension within the team. Some felt offended that they weren't offered the position, since they had been with the company for years and had more experience. They could tell I had none, so why was I brought in instead of promoting from within? The truth was, the Librería General didn't sign me on to pay for my learning curve—I was supposed to already be an expert. Given the state of my skill set, my contribution didn't go beyond that of a standard sales agent.

Six months later, I was fired. This was not unexpected. I hadn't achieved any of the outcomes that were set at the start. I wasn't ready to step in at the director level. But I did have something constructive to share with the CEO, which I knew he would most likely not want to hear.

This CEO was not approachable. His office door was almost always closed, only permitting people in when he wanted to either fire or yell at them. I knocked anyway.

"Sir, fair enough that you're firing me. I was actually expecting this. However, I would ask for just five minutes of your valuable time."

"Ah! Why are you not surprised that I've fired you?"

We'd always enjoyed a friendly connection, so I pressed on with what I wanted to say.

"When you hired me, the consulting agency you used was highly professional, but I genuinely believe that the system they used did not match what you were looking for. I am sorry to say it, but the program is completely inaccurate."

"What do you mean? Why is that? They are one of the best consulting agencies in the area."

"Sir, I am not saying they aren't good at what they do. But I was able to successfully get through the written assessment by literally guessing at my answers 75 percent of the time. I have to assume that they don't fully understand your business and that their assessment is really a psychological test on behavior and competencies, rather than being personalized.

"My being selected as the best candidate for the job proves this. I believe that your human resources manager needs to meet with this consulting agency and make sure they understand the needs of your organization, not just the position. You have great people already on board here, many of whom are capable of achieving exactly what you're looking for. You need a way to discover that talent. I did my best to be a director, but I wasn't ready for the position."

Just as I expected, he was less than pleased to hear this feedback. "You should have told me from the beginning that you didn't feel you were capable," he replied, "then I wouldn't have wasted both time and money on you."

"I agree, I should have been honest. I am approaching you now because I learned from that mistake, and what I'm trying to do now I'm hoping will save you money and help you achieve your goals more effectively."

"I'm listening, but you only have five minutes."

I told him to first freeze the retainer he held with the consulting agency. Ask the human resources manager to present an action plan. Then, decide whether to continue with the external agency or terminate that contract. I pointed out that the rotation rate was high, and that competitors were stealing the best employees because they were being overlooked for advancement. I said that when the internal customer is set up for failure, it's impossible for them to deliver exceptional service and build a sense of loyalty.

He was even less pleased to hear this.

"It's my products and my location, not my people, that have made me successful," he countered.

"I agree you have a great location and outstanding products, but you're missing the point in how you deliver outstanding service. How can your organization be successful without great people behind it?"

This, surprisingly, garnered a more positive reaction. And an invitation to lunch. Truthfully, I had been trying to assuage my own guilt in not living up to expectations, but I decided to run with this. I asked if he would invite the human resources manager to lunch with us since she was the only person who was able to give him an accurate picture of his internal customers and answer any questions. I stressed that as a top manager on the team, she needed to be within his circle of trust. He accepted this suggestion, and the three of us went for lunch.

Our lunch meeting began with the CEO expressing his doubt in firing me, now that he's heard my ideas. I was appreciative, but I wanted to get through what I had in store for this lunch and deliver a return on investment for the six months I'd already been in his employ. And to do this, I needed the human resources manager.

She courageously shared the belief that people come first, but at their library, people seemed to come last. Neither the products nor the location could outperform an associate's attitude. And they couldn't continue to operate as though everything was an emergency that demanded to be addressed immediately—a comprehensive plan would be more effective. She suggested that if they wanted to retain their internal customers and exceed their financial numbers, they needed to work with their associates to find undiscovered talents.

"So what do you have in mind?" the CEO asked.

"If we assemble an internal group for recruitment, we would be able to personalize the interview based on our specific needs, experience, and what we believe the organization needs in order to make the team more productive," she replied.

I thought it was a wonderful idea and said so. They would basically be grooming an internal consultant, instead of paying an external company. The budget to achieve the outcomes would stay within the company and the associates would feel appreciated.

The CEO did express doubts. What if the company didn't have the people they needed already on the team? The human resources manager assured him that this was not the case, and if anyone required additional preparation then training in that skill could easily be arranged.

The CEO then asked why he was only learning about all of this now. Why not earlier, when certain challenges could have been avoided? Again with courage, the human resources manager explained that his unapproachable manner discouraged anyone from trying to speak with him, especially when ideas might not be well received. This bit of information really opened the CEO's mind to just how close-minded he had been. But he was still resisting any need for change. He'd been successful so far, hadn't he?

The human resources manager was able to navigate this potentially sticky point by shifting the focus away from the CEO changing as a person toward learning how to adapt to new market demands. She asked for his trust in the team, and for permission for them to be empowered as decision-makers and to take agency over their own professional development.

This sounded better to the CEO. A bit more manageable. But what next?

This was where the point about people coming first came into play. The human resources manager emphasized that they needed to pay attention to the organization, and to the people who showed up each day with confidence and a positive attitude, hungry to learn and grow, full of passion and integrity.

"Paying attention? What do you mean by that?" the CEO asked. "I believe that since they're earning good money, we never stopped paying attention to them, so I disagree."

This is where I stepped in.

"Sir, let me use my case as an example. I took the position of sales director, and then I had zero guidelines from you. You were nice in celebrating my hire with champagne, asking me to make you money, but you didn't help me understand your vision and why you wanted to open the international market. When I asked for the details behind how you envisioned the 30 percent increase in sales the first year, you answered that it was up to me. You hired me to tell you how to do it."

I wasn't giving excuses for my failure; I was telling him that no matter how great he was at his job, his associates need a regularly scheduled refresher on the vision of the CEO and a clear understanding of the direction the company is heading.

I asked him if he realized that he already had a strong human resources manager, who possessed the know-how to manage a consultant and produce the desired results. He was coming around to see my way of thinking.

"Johnny, why don't you stay and assist our human resources manager in improving her department, and build something new. I believe you can grow into a great director," he said.

I was flattered and relieved that I was helpful in the end, but I couldn't accept the offer.

"Sir, wise recruitment and a prepared associate will take your organization to the next level you're striving for, and with this approach, your level of service and customer loyalty will improve significantly, and you don't even need me to be involved."

We shook hands, and he promised to inform me in another six months' time if what he had invested in me proved to be worth it. I became a loyal customer for the library, rather than an employee. Two months later, I received an invitation to an event: the first party held at Librería General since opening their doors twenty years ago.

There, they surprised me with a free membership at the library for two years and a 10 percent discount on any purchase for life. They gifted all two hundred employees with the same that day as well. This gesture was so moving to me, saying to everyone as I thanked them that although I had failed at the position I'd held, I learned from being a rookie, and walked away more enriched than I could have ever imagined.

This experience from start to end is one I will never forget. The lesson behind sharing this story is that we need to be able to detect internal talent, and not miss potential by immediately looking for solutions outside the organization. Talented and loyal people are the backbone of the success of your company.

As someone in a leadership position, we too often waste time complaining about what's not working among our employers, rather than noticing and supporting the growth of our top talent. Do not just speak about underperforming or negative employees; take action. It takes a great leader to build a great team, and one lousy link in the chain is enough to break it.

Too many leaders make hires without being aware of the potential they already have inside their organization. Your mission is to consider those leaders, managers, and associates on your team who possess the talent and empower them to become not only ambassadors of your company culture, but also champions of discovering talent from within their own teams.

More Current Recruitment Strategies

That's how things happened in the 1990s. Now let's compare it with more contemporary recruitment strategies.

In 2017, I was hired as a project coordinator for a massive hiring initiative with Marina Bay Hotel in in Mallorca, Spain. The call came from Fatima Alcantara, the guest experience director for the Spanish region.

"Johnny, I have great news," she said, "Melía Hotels International has won the competition for managing the Palau de Congressos de Palma and its annex hotel."

The Palau de Congressos de Palma (Palma Convention Center) is a world-class conference venue, complete with full-service conference facilities, versatile high-level service, and the perfect balance between technology, design, and cost-effectiveness for both business and leisure.

"I'm calling because we need you to design a strategy for the large-scale recruitment that will be required. We need something that will deliver a positive message, since everyone from the Balearic government, ministry of tourism, the press, our competitors, tour operators, and travel agencies will be watching this project unfold."

I was all in. I was quick in my decision to accept this role, and given my positive track record working with Melía Hotels International, confident in our ability to succeed. Over the preceding ten years, the company had hired me as part of task forces for the pre-opening of properties to assist with recruitment and the interview process. And as a customer experience designer, I was well-versed in helping various companies with their recruitment process in a multitude of countries.

I was on a flight from Miami to Mallorca the day after that phone call with Fatima to visit the hotel, learn about the facilities, and brainstorm the vision for how we could create something spectacular. My primary objective was to make the process as stress-free as possible. I wanted the experience to be enjoyable, to be memorable because it was fun, and to ensure a level of excellence for all involved. I wanted candidates to understand that the company's priority was to hire people they believed were able to create a customer experience that went beyond the quality of the accommodation.

This is what I envisioned the process to look like.

The candidate experience would start with a hostess welcome at the group recruitment reception, where each person will receive a program that outlined next steps and instructions on how to connect with the interviewers. Interviewers would greet the candidates and provide them with iPads that held a questionnaire, as well as information on the positions that were available and the competencies required for each specific role. The candidates would have one hour with the iPad—from 5:00 to 6:00 p.m. —with the assistance of the interviewers for support.

The idea behind the questionnaire and filling it out with the help of the interviewers was to break the ice and make the candidates feel welcome. It also would help candidates feel like part of the company from the start, helping to avoid potential bureaucratic red tape should they be hired. I wanted their first day of work to be focused on meeting their peers and learning about the job and responsibilities, not filling out paperwork.

The first meeting room at the recruitment event would be decorated with projected images and videos that best represented the company's values and attributes. These messages would serve a dual purpose as prompts for the interviewers to question candidates during the one-on-one interactions. I wanted to ensure that candidates were interested and engaged with their surroundings, as well as provide a starting point for the interviewers. I even wanted a DJ to be playing chilled-out music in the hall and the brand's signature scent perfuming every room to complete the ambiance.

We had one hundred candidates and twelve interviewers moving through the experience I designed for them that day. Each candidate was required to pass through five stages in groups, which were divided by color and assigned at the main entrance.

Stage one was team building. In this stage, I focused on creating interactions, asking candidates to take Polaroid pictures of one another and hang them under their group color posted on a wall. Each person was instructed to then write one positive thing they had noticed about the others, and post that below the respective photos.

The purpose was to emphasize that we as a company were looking for people who were open-minded, willing to work with others, and able to communicate and connect in a positive way. If at the end of this recruitment process a candidate was hired, their picture and the positive notes would be posted to the human resources mood board wall at the hotel. If a candidate's application was unsuccessful, they would have the option to take their photos home as a souvenir.

Stage two involved role playing. The members of each colored group sat together before two interviewers and would play-act based on a specific service. This service could be resolving a complaint, or doing a check-in or check-out, up-selling or cross-selling, and so on. The interviewer took notes, observing each candidate and noticing how that person thought, moved, listened, and interacted.

The candidates were evaluated on their attitude, decision-making skills, and expertise in service. All of these notes were recorded in a folder—one for each candidate—that was passed to the interviewers at the next stage. The interviewers' mission was to fill these folders with insights on the performance of the candidates.

After the role-playing, the groups moved on to a waiting room, where they had the option to enjoy finger foods, listen to music, relax, or speak to someone from the human resources department about any questions.

Stage three introduced the one-to-two interviews. A member of the human resources team was present to connect each candidate with a representative of the department they were most interested in and would sit in on the meeting. If a candidate passed through this stage, the chances of a successful hire were more than 80 percent.

Stage four was the closing. This was the one-on-one interview between a candidate and human resources to ensure a good fit for the job and to determine availability and salary.

Stage five involved a site inspection for approved candidates only. The commercial team provided an on-site tour for those hired, modeled to reflect the same experience as a customer. The new hires learned about the hotel offers and attributes, how the sales department promotes each of the other departments, and how to add value.

And this was the element designed to surprise. A week before the new associates were scheduled to begin their new positions, they each received a personalized video with instructions on where to pick up their new uniform, the guidelines for how to wear it, details on where they were expected to report, and at what time, and the names of the team members who would be waiting for them upon arrival. At the end of these videos was a short message from their individual manager directly to each new associate, welcoming them to the team and offering encouragement for success.

The idea behind going this extra mile was to exceed their expectations before they even started working, demonstrating the culture and values so they could experience them firsthand, therefore increasing their desire to work at this specific hotel.

The press and government representatives were involved throughout this entire large-scale recruitment process, having been invited to experience each of the five stages. They were able to witness the incredible success we had in recruiting highly talented people and making a difference in each and every step of the way. We achieved our goal of making an impact.

Two years later, the hotel had a staff rotation rate of less than 20 percent, a significant reduction from the standard 50 to 60 percent seen with a typical new business opening, particularly in the hotel industry. The experience created during the recruitment process is the difference maker here, and how the new associates fell in love with and committed to the brand even before their first day on the job. And, of course, credit must go to the leaders of the company and how they managed this project, and their belief in their associates.

None of this is to say the hiring process was a walk in the park, just because the experience was designed to create a connection. The interview process was rigorous, with aggressive questions meant to secure the best candidates.

Many leaders ask me, do interviews have to be aggressive? The answer is yes. Aggressive questions are one of the crucial components of the success of your recruitment strategy. What I mean by this is that questions should be unexpected, and you must apply pressure to the interviewee to see how they react, and if they can handle it. This way you'll know whether or not they can work under pressure. If you are opening a new business, this ability to handle oneself well in stressful situations will be essential.

This doesn't mean that you should behave in an aggressive manner toward your candidates. You can use your questions to be direct, and ask for pointed information. For example, you could ask a candidate to tell you about a disappointment or disagreement they had with a superior, and the eventual outcome of that situation. You could ask an interviewee to name three bad behaviors of a previous boss, or three occasions they were criticized. The purpose behind these types of questions is to gauge how candidates respond, if they remain positive or become uncomfortable, and whether or not they pass positive or negative judgments on others.

You want your candidates to be engaged before being selected, and you want to make the selection process memorable. Your job is to impact all in a positive way, discover potential among the candidates, and hire those people. Treat every prospective team member as you would a real customer, regardless of whether you end up hiring them or not. Turn interviews into auditions that provide you not only with the information you need, but also with an experience that creates a lasting memory for all involved. They might indeed become part of your team, or they just might become a customer.

Questions

Build the script of an all-star cast. By answering, sharing, and printing those questions and answers, you will help the human resources department and recruitment force build a script to detect and improve the recruitment system. Do you look for positive attitude people as recruiters? Or just an excellent CV? How do you recognize a positive attitude?

Do you have a questionnaire based on the values and culture of your organization? Write down three examples.

Are you detecting at your organization those talented candidates who can become managers or leaders? How and why do you consider them to be talented? Write eight to ten behaviors or habits that would make you consider those candidates for a higher position.

Never stop talented people from advancing because they are right where they are, and you are afraid of moving them to the next level to avoid making a hole where they are now. Instead, encourage those talented people that you don't want to move to the next position to become a trainer. Train a possible candidate to replace them and that will give them the opportunity to grow and help you as a leader to make sure that you are not letting down any position. Think about what other options you can offer those potential positions that will help them move to the next level.

Hiring is a vital part. But it is just a start. Are you making your hiring day memorable? Write down your strategy: What are you doing to make your internal customers tick every day and keep them on track? Write down four ideas.

Is making the first day on the job the best day experience for new employees? Or they are filling out paperwork all day long? Do not, under any circumstances, hide talented associates and limit their growth. Instead, be the first one to promote them and help them succeed. Also consider the following in your recruitment:

- Offer excellent onboarding training to keep employees loyal to your organization.
- Make your recruitment day memorable.
- Be creative and exceed expectations. They might become your employee or your customer.
- Make talented people part of your recruitment team.
- Motivate them to become better.
- Before you hire external associates, promote from inside your organization and see who raises their hand to help. Conduct interviews internally before doing so externally and if they do not have the profile and competencies you are looking for, let them know the reason and ask them if they desire the position.
- Put these employees into development to achieve their goals.
- Do not ignore them because they are good. They could become your worst employees.
- Help them to make it happen and monitor them, show interest in their future and development.
- Encourage them to keep going and not to let go.
- Invest time in recruitment and break any rules of bureaucracy.
- Conduct interviews with the support of others. Do not use the one-to-one interview by phone. Have someone with you who has the same beliefs but a different way of management or even staff in growth projection. This can be beneficial for interviews. Doing this will also help you see prospective hires from a different perspective.

Asking the right questions will help you discover those people especially in the era we live in today. People today need to understand your purpose, and you need to understand theirs too. So ask them about their purpose and share yours. Assessment tests should never be based merely on behaviors, but also on the values of the organization.

The Essence of the Script

You don't want just good people working for you. You want *great people*. To achieve that goal, follow a method of selection based on your beliefs-values and what you stand for as an organization. How do you select the right people? The right people always hold the key to the success of your organization. Many organizations have a prototype of competencies or an established assessment that they follow. Others hire headhunters to select their people.

The question is what is the right way to get great people.Many leaders forget that talented people who work long, hard hours might lose their passion and get burned out. They may also be suffering from:

- Having few resources
- Feeling under pressure
- Feeling there are too many demands
- Feeling dispensable
- Feeling guilty if they go home early
- Feeling underpaid
- Feeling abandoned

Design a company culture you can describe in one simple sentence. Then, you will deliver superior customer experiences with ease.

5

Customer Experience Begins with a Harmonious Team

Y ou will not get far without building a team with an inner core of positive energy, regardless of how much pressure you apply. Your customer experience results are dependent on everyone within your company being on board with your objectives. As a leader, you want each member of your team to learn any challenges your organization faces as well as understand your vision, purpose, and goals in order to create a sense of harmony. Then, with a harmonious team, your customer experience strategy will be achieved.

Yet there is always room for improvement. Most of my clients struggle to bond the leaders of their own organizations together and to create this sense of harmony and positivity from the top down. There's also a challenge in convincing management to accept this concept. For these reasons, the best way to start is with the culture of the brand.

In the chapter about your associates being the heartbeat of your organization, you learned about the power of culture. But culture alone is not enough. Introducing a new culture is the first step toward the success of your customer experience strategy—the next challenge lies in maintaining that culture.

My objective is always for everyone within an organization to think, believe, talk and behave in sync. This is what I mean by being in harmony. Too often I see smaller cliques at play within a company that are operating separately from the greater organization. The leaders of these cliques care only about themselves, and their department, and have little concern for what anyone else is doing. This is a gross misunderstanding of the real meaning of culture, and of leadership and team management.

Before I start designing a customer experience strategy for any client I work with, my first goal is to identify and start to break apart those cliques. I then align them with the direction the company as a whole is moving toward and then install in them a belief in the experience we will be creating for both the internal and external customers. I open the door for them to accept change.

Often, leaders, management, and associates fear change. New things are coming, which is exciting, but at the same time can be scary. Often they don't believe in it. Then they start gossiping about the changes and criticizing new ideas, which only wastes time. They believe that since they have been a hotel for ages, and you are a newcomer, you can't possibly know what will work on their property. The fear is often palpable in the environment, and clearly visible in the demeanor and performance of the team members.

This was one of the challenges I faced at that property in Cancún, as I shared in the heartbeat chapter. I felt the fear of change from within that team and saw it on everyone's faces. I could see it in their performance. I wasn't surprised, as the prospect of change is often unwelcome news for internal customers. The idea causes a shift in energy on the job, emerging as fear, criticism, false judgment, insecurity, inefficiency, loss of motivation, and distraction.

I knew I must address this at its root cause. I had to think in reverse and imagine what the outcome would be once the changes were already implemented. By jumping ahead to the end result, I would be able to describe the success to the team and help them imagine so they could see it for themselves. That was my big moment of clarity: focusing on the why instead of the how because uncertainty over the how gives rise to doubt. A strong belief in the why overcomes those doubts.

I decided not to announce that new changes were coming. Instead, I wanted to celebrate our success, before it even happened. I wanted to instill belief that our success was inevitable, and operate from that place. I wanted to eliminate the word *change* from our vocabulary, and create a sense of team-work by encouraging associates' visions, and their ideas on how to achieve them.

The project in Cancún was by far the most successful in my more than twenty years of experience as a hotelier leader. For a project to excel, I need to feel a sense of a team working in harmony and living the change through their own effort and achievement. Always, the question in my mind revolves around joining any cliques within an organization so all parties are working together. This requires a shift in thinking away from celebrating individual success and snickering at the failure of others, and toward operating in sync with a greater attachment to the brand as a whole.

If I am able to influence a team to work in harmony, understand the changes that are being made, and believe in the power of the new customer experience concept, then my first battle is over. Once I help a team see themselves as pioneers of the project and take ownership on behalf of the entire company, then I consider my work to be a success.

To achieve this in Cancún, I started by asking questions. I needed to understand whether or not everyone was on the same page. The questions may have been simple, but they were designed to help me see the big picture for both the operational and executive teams. An anonymous survey gave me all of the information I needed:

- Are you willing to be successful?
- Do you believe and feel that you can be part of the new brand?
- Are willing to do things that are outside your comfort zone?
- Do you enjoy working here?
- Do you like your team?
- What would you do if you were the general manager?

The responses I received were positive, which provided a great starting point for that project.

When you ask these questions, you'll begin to see patterns. It is not unusual at this point to identify the small groups that are working separately, and are operating under a different mindset than the rest of the organization. Often you'll see that the behavior of the leaders and managers is focused on themselves, and their departments, and that they have less concern for others. This presents difficulty in implementing a new customer experience concept because the real meaning of leadership and working as a team is misunderstood.

It becomes my task to get these individuals on board and help them believe in the concept of the project before I start designing a new customer experience strategy. My goal is always to break apart any small organizations, and get them aligned to our mission by buying into the potential of the experience we can create for both the internal and external customer. I want all team members to bond, begin to work together, break any habits that aren't serving the desired outcome, and embrace change.

This bonding ideally happens before a project has even been implemented.

My first objective in achieving this is to break up routines.

One idea for achieving this was inspired by a Brazilian party I once attended. At that party, I loved how connected the group was to each other, and how the performance by the entertainers there was built to include everyone. An idea popped into my mind, and I wanted those musicians in on it. I asked if I could hire them to teach a team I was working with at the time how to create a percussion show without a musical instrument. My team could use anything that made a sound, just not a traditional instrument. The musicians said they would do it.

Back on site for my project, I shared this idea with the team. The reactions were mixed, the first being outright rejection (those would be the No-Nos) and questioning the purpose of this endeavor and how it mattered.

"This is a waste of our time. We have too much to do to be playing music."

"I can't play an instrument, so why is Johnny asking us to do this?"

My reply to these questions was that I wanted to ensure that everyone was one band.

"But Johnny, we are already one team; why would having us play music help us perform better?"

I was honest with my reply. I told them that each of them was great at what they did as individuals, but they were not great at what they did together. I told them I needed them to trust the process and give their team a chance for even more success. I gave each person the choice of which "instrument" to play, which in turn gave them the opportunity to think creatively. I also informed the group that in forty-five days from that date they would be performing, on stage, in front of 250 tour operators and sales managers at the first gala dinner to promote the hotel brand worldwide. And they would have just forty minutes a day to practice.

My aim was to build a team that worked together to succeed and create a sense of belonging. I dared them, letting them know that I would be part of every single rehearsal. I didn't make it mandatory, but rather encouraged and made the challenge clear.

The training was a mess at the start. Four team members decided to quit during the first week because they didn't believe in their ability to achieve the goal. They were afraid of failing. And the first week was lousy—noise, more than music. But slowly, those who stuck with it started listening to each other and finding a common beat. They started to improve, which led to a sense of excitement.

Instead of practicing just forty minutes a day during their shift, the decision was made to practice more after work hours. I began to see the band members start to build themselves up and grow as a cohesive team by helping each other grasp the beat and the rhythm. They scheduled extra rehearsals on the weekends. They were transforming into a great team because the music was bringing them together.

I witnessed the team power through ten signs:

- They were having fun and enjoying the journey.
- They were showing respect for each other instead of criticizing mistakes.
- They were putting their individual goals second to the team's goals.
- They embraced changes and accepted something new and different.
- They were humble.
- They understood the meaning of strengthening as a team

because they felt the beat and could see that when the
music was good, motivation increased.
- They started projecting a positive attitude.
- They were hungry to learn and get better.
- They were building trust.
- They encouraged the four team members who quit in the
  beginning to rejoin and helped them catch up to the
  point that those four members became among the best in
  the band.

On December 5 of that year we hosted a holiday party for our
internal customers. This was thirty-five days after the start of the
band, and I thought they were ready for their first appearance
before performing in front of the tour operators and sales
managers at the gala. My team's performance would be a gift
from the managers to the employees. The performance turned
out to be a resounding success, which sent a strong message to
the other internal customers on the power of team bonding.

On December 15, we performed at the gala. We wowed our audience with our creativity, and even more so when we presented
the team players. It was at this moment that I saw my team's
tears of joy as they shared their experience of the band experi-
ment. At first, none could see the purpose behind the idea, but
now they got it. They realized that they did something memorable. And customer experience is all about creating memories.

The team realized that they not only connected emotionally, but
also proved to the tour operators, sales agencies, and even to
themselves what is possible, even when in their minds initially
they believed it to be impossible. I told them that now they
understood the meaning and the power of creating experiences.
Each member grew as a leader within the team, as each could see
the effort put into acting as one team, working toward one goal,
with one belief. Now they were ready to embrace the new

customer experience concept because they had just lived what creating experiences are all about.

I was at that hotel in December of that year to deliver training on service culture for the associates. The property was undergoing an ownership and brand change, from Hilton Iguazú to Meliá Iguazú. During this training session, I asked the participants if they remembered a time when they felt like a harmonious team, all working together toward the same purpose and goal, and if they have ever been able to truly wow a customer. I also asked whether or not they had ever been wowed themselves. I wanted to know if they ever felt they had succeeded in creating an extraordinary customer experience, and why they felt it was a success.

A bellboy, Alberto Villalba, replied with this story. The previous year, the Gutierrez family visited the hotel for five nights to experience the Iguazú Falls. Mr. Gutierrez, who came with his wife and three adult children, was overweight and confined to a wheelchair. The hotel, a Hilton property, is situated on a cliff-top, which offers views of these extraordinary falls. The terrain is not suited to traversing via a wheelchair.

Each morning, Mr. Gutierrez and his family would go to breakfast and sit at a table that was specially assigned to accommodate his wheelchair and his large size. On the first day, following breakfast, the family went on an excursion to explore the falls. Everyone except Mr. Gutierrez, that is. The father sat outside on the terrace of the restaurant while his family experienced these majestic falls, and he waited for them to return since he could not walk.

Alberto shared that all the bellboys empathized with Mr. Gutierrez. They knew his needs, his likes, and dislikes, when he preferred to eat and drink, and even which newspapers he enjoyed reading. "Everyone at the hotel was informed of Mr.

Gutierrez's needs, and we wanted him to feel at home," he explained to me.

Alberto said that on the second day of the family's stay, he asked Mr. Gutierrez if he would like to visit the falls. He told him that the team would find a solution to make it possible. Mr. Gutierrez replied that he would love to go with his family and live the experience himself. Alberto offered to take the experience one step further and make this excursion a surprise to the rest of the Gutierrez family. Mr. Gutierrez was delighted by this prospect.

The bellboy team, maintenance team, housekeeping team, and managers all banded together to create a safe, comfortable solution to this dream come true for Mr. Gutierrez. Maintenance was able to modify a bellboy cart with sturdier wheels that could hold more weight, and side panels that made a sort of "car" with doors. Housekeeping provided a large pillow for added comfort. By using this customized cart and having two bellboys and an associate to accompany him, the hotel team made it possible for Mr. Gutierrez to surprise his family and join their tour that day.

This gesture brought tears to the eyes of the family and hotel team alike, so touching a moment it was. For Mr. Gutierrez, it was easily one of the happiest days of his life, and even the retelling of this story by Alberto one year late had the power to bring tears to my own eyes. This was a powerful example of a harmonious team, and I told the group so.

The team harmony in this instance created a memorable experience that exceeded the expectation of the customer in every aspect. The team accepted a challenge and faced it with innovation, making adjustments outside the usual scope of their day, and this effort motivated everyone involved to work together to achieve the desired outcome. No one was hindered by negative thinking. They made the decision to go for it, and the results followed. They had the support, trust, and empowerment of management, and that was the key component of their success.

The Gutierrez family became loyal supporters and ambassadors for the hotel. That modified bellboy cart is still in use, and has been further improved and personalized for Mr. Gutierrez.

This is the potential that's within reach when you have a harmonious team. It is essential to share your vision with all your teams, without forcing the word *change* upon them, and to ask about their own visions and whether or not they believe in their ability to achieve them. If you make your team members part of the idea, you can encourage a sense of ownership. Let them take credit for it, and watch as their excitement grows.

Then, focus on introducing new ideas and concepts that will make an impact while shifting the team philosophy as you work towards goals step by step. You can accomplish all of this with less resistance by omitting the word *change* from your rhetoric.

When teams work in harmony, they have more fun, they care about each other more, and they perform at a higher level. By bringing harmony into your teams you will excel in delivering an unparalleled customer experience.

Questions

List three or more areas you have noticed about your team that could use reinforcing in order to develop harmony.

Brainstorm with your team to come up with new ways of building harmony. Doing some role playing might be the most efficient way to track those that have the most efficacy. Describe the top three below.

What are some ways you could integrate more fun into current team practices? How can you begin implementing these right away?

Comfort is the enemy of growth. Take one action every day that pushes you into discomfort and transforms from the inside out.

6

Deliver a Performance
Customers Will Never Forget

How many times have you called your best friend or approached a coworker and said, "You won't believe what happened to me just now"? These words usually precede a story about something bad that happened, right? And then when you tell the story, you upset your listener —and further upset yourself. Here's my challenge for us as customer experience designers: let's take back the phrase *you won't believe what happened* from negative situations, and use it instead for positive moments like these:

- Moments that make us smile and laugh
- Moments that warm our hearts
- Moments that surprise us
- Moments worth celebrating
- Moments worth telling stories about, year after year, to everyone we meet
- Moments that interrupt the humdrum of daily life and introduce novelty and excitement
- Moments we remember for a lifetime but feel like they happened only yesterday

As customer experience designers, it is our job to create such moments—Happenings, as I call them—for everyone who encounters our brand. We must go above and beyond to keep both new and loyal customers satisfied. And when we do, we can leave our competitors far behind.

For this chapter, I have chosen six stories, each illustrating a different element of what I've named the Happenings Approach so you can create similar moments in your own life and in the lives of your customers. The six elements are:

- Reaching customers on a soul level
- A sense of ownership
- Bold action and execution
- The "wow" factor
- A sense of mystery and surprise
- Creating story-worthy experiences

Each story will help you master the elements individually. By the end of the chapter, you will know how to integrate all six into every Happening you create, so that you can boost brand recognition and increase revenue.

Reaching Customers on a Soul Level

Think back to your experiences as a customer. Has there ever been a company that provided you with a service that shook you to your core, that reached your very soul?

Every time I teach a workshop, I ask participants this question. And every time, I am met with silence. Why? Because reaching the soul of a customer—providing services and experiences that reach all the way to the soul level—is a rarity. It almost never happens. But it should, because these experiences become something customers will never forget.

Imagine reaching the soul level of just 10 percent of your customers. Imagine witnessing the emotional impact you would make. Your energy would increase, right? As would your revenue. And you'd put that energy and capital back into your brand during prosperous times, and save it for security during less prosperous times. In addition, your team will feel inspired to deliver more experiences that reach the souls of 50 percent of your customers. Then 75 percent. Then every one of them.

In March 2019, I traveled to Barcelona to train a hotel's staff on how to take service from competent to excellent. After a nonstop day of working, teaching, and creating, I set out to have a drink. My goal was to disconnect from the grind and relax before going to bed.

I went across the street and found a small beer bar. I couldn't see a name from the outside—it seemed like a nondescript spot—but it looked cozy through the window and the customers seemed to be at ease. I was on the fence about going in, since beer isn't really my taste, but the longer I stood outside, the cozier this place looked and the happier the customers looked. Before I could tell myself to move on and keep looking for a place that was more my style, I was opening the door and sliding onto a stool at the bar.

The bartender approached me within seconds of sitting down, a smile on his face.

"I am Diego. What is your name?"

"I'm Johnny."

"Nice meeting you, Johnny. I'll be your beer sommelier this evening. Here's the menu. Let me know if I can assist you with anything."

I took a quick glance up and down the menu. I had no idea what to get.

"Diego, I have to confess something."

"What's that, Johnny?'"

"I am not a beer fan. Can you recommend something to me?"

"Have you ever had a beer that you liked? Or a flavor?"

"I used to order golden beer, but it didn't have a soft flavor."

Diego then gave me a rundown of the varieties and origins of his golden beers and suggested that I taste a sample of each one so that I could experience their qualities firsthand.

"The complexity of a beer," he said, "is in its flavors and sensations. When you drink it, you have to ask yourself, *how does this feel in my mouth?*"

Already, Diego was transforming my attitude toward beer. Never before had I thought about the sensation in my mouth— only the taste.

"If you feel two or more taste sensations or flavors on your palate," he continued, "that means the beer is complex."

"What kind of sensations do you mean?"

"Warm, dry, bubbly, sweet, creamy, heavy, or soft. Anything like those, or whatever comes to your mind."

I was getting excited and brought the glass to my mouth to take a sip and try Diego's method.

"Wait, wait!" he exclaimed. "Not yet."

The beer had almost touched my lips, but I pulled the glass away fast.

"Why not?"

"Because," said Diego, "before drinking the beer you have to awaken your sense of smell. The aroma of the beer is what helps you identify the complexity and the quality. Okay?"

"Okay."

"*Now*, take a sip and swirl the beer around in your mouth before swallowing it."

I did as he instructed.

"You will discover many flavors," he said as I swirled, "like toast, nuts, caramel, floral, herbal, maybe a spice or fruit flavor."

For a moment, all I detected was deliciousness, but then a few distinct flavors emerged.

"Can you tell?" he asked, just as I was swallowing.

"Yes, I taste caramel and nuts. I can detect nuts easily because I am a nuts lover. It's like eating caramel nuts."

"Do you know what that means?"

I shook my head.

"If you can detect some flavors, you can become a beer expert and lover."

The way he presented each flavor and its value piqued my curiosity. I found myself asking a lot of questions about craft beer, different flavors and qualities. After half an hour, I felt like my life had changed.

"Diego, I want to ask you another question."

"Sure!"

"What is the difference between a wine sommelier and beer sommelier?"

"Wine," he said, "depends on the year and what's going on in nature. Beer has to be designed with a creative mind and taste. The process of brewing is like cooking a dish that delights and enriches your palate in every bite. Both wine and beer are works of art."

Such a beautiful answer he gave. I polished off two beers and then Diego presented me to his colleague, Gabriela.

"Hello, Johnny, I am your cocktail stylist. How is your beer?"

Holy moly! First a beer sommelier, and then a cocktail stylist? This place was unreal.

"The beer is excellent. This is turning out to be my night. With your help I'll get drunk and recover completely from jet lag," I laughed. "I would love a cocktail."

"Wonderful!" she said. "What are your three favorite drinks, starting at the top?"

"Sake, red wine, and tequila."

"And your favorite two flowers?"

Strange question.

"Jasmine and gardenia. My father loves those flowers and used to tell me they were flowers of purity, with the scent of love."

Gabriela smiled. "Would you like to try a gardenia sake sour?" she asked.

"Yes, absolutely."

Watching Gabriela craft the cocktail with my favorite flower, I then understood why she calls herself a cocktail stylist. She has a special touch and glamour that made the process like a show.

The sake sour she made was mixed gardenia with sugar and featured a gardenia flower on top. The smell of the flower brought memories of my father to mind. I could feel my soul awakening at this moment.

When she handed me the drink, the flavor and texture were unbelievable. I finished the gardenia sake sour and promptly ordered another one before returning to the hotel.

The next evening, at the end of my journey, I returned to the bar with two managers of the hotel. On my way in, Gabriela approached me and said, "Johnny, I found some jasmine and Diego and I would like to make you a beer cocktail featuring it. We're calling it 'Jas-sense.'"

"Yes, of course! I've never tasted a beer cocktail."

As soon as the drink was in my hand and passing over my lips, the Jas-sense brought tears to my eyes. I remembered summers with my father and how much he loved jasmine trees.

"Do you do this with every customer?" I asked her.

"I listen to every customer and make sure they live one moment here that they will remember. If there is an ingredient I don't have in a particular moment, I always make sure to have it the next day," she replied.

More tears welled up in my eyes at the memory of my father, and at what I was absorbing from my experience in this bar with no name. It was staffing itself with experts in their field—people who are willing to find out what every customer loves, improve what they create, and even create new things. Everyone knows how to make a sake sour but she put soul into the cocktail and transformed a simple cocktail into a Happening that I would never forget.

Gabriela made the extra effort to find a jasmine flower, even though, as her customer, I never indicated that I would return. In doing so, she and Diego created a Happening, reaching my very soul.

And it all started with asking a few questions.

Before I left, she wrote the cocktail recipes on two coasters, along with the dates I was there and gave them to me as a souvenir. Then, she took a picture to record her creativity.

I spent the rest of the week's worth of workshops showing pictures of the cocktails and talking about the Happenings both Diego and Gabriela provided. I left Barcelona with my soul awakened and with a memory that will live on forever.

Now you're probably thinking, "That's great for bars, but I am in a completely different industry. How can I create Happenings that reach my customers on a soul level?"

No matter what kind of service, product, or experience you offer, your job is to invite your customers into *your* expertise, just like Diego did, rather than keeping it for yourself.

What is your specialized knowledge? How can you teach it to customers in a way that is interactive and fun?

In addition, you need to be the storyteller for every experience. Find out one piece of your customer's story and integrate those details into your interaction with the customer, just as Gabriela did. Link those details to the way your customer encounters the product or service you offer.

Stories cement experience into memory, while transferring expertise enriches everyone's soul.

Be sure to hire innovative experts and position them on the front lines of customer interaction. Empower them to create Happenings, with your support. Then watch your team propel your brand to the next level by recruiting customers for life.

A Sense of Ownership

Many companies have loyalty programs. No doubt you're on the list for dozens of them. *Click here for 20 percent off. Sign up below to receive your free gift. Shop this Saturday for MEGA savings. Happy birthday! Enjoy 15 percent off your order from our latest collection.* And more.

And what do you get in return for signing up? A mailbox stuffed with fliers and an inbox cluttered with endless offers. Your loyalty just means you've given a company permission to put your information in a big database and send you and every other customer the same avalanche of junk. Is this the way to keep your loyalty? Probably not. These companies will probably lose that loyalty at some point and never understand why.

When I worked retail, managing thirteen fashion boutiques, I wanted to dispense with the typical loyalty programs and create something new, a loyalty experience for customers that felt fresh and exciting. I wanted to turn loyalty experiences into Happenings.

I called it the ten-second owner program. If you, as the customer, spent a certain dollar amount within a one-year period, you could *own* the entire store for ten whole seconds online, on the date and time of your choosing. During that time you'd choose whatever garment, pair of shoes, accessory, or other merchandise you liked—and it would be yours, no extra charge.

I did put into place a few rules to ensure that the boutiques, as well as the customers, were taken care of:

- Your selection must not exceed the highest dollar amount you've spent with the boutique.
- Your selection is final.
- You cannot exchange the selection for money.

Did this idea work? Absolutely! Most customers could identify exactly what they wanted, and when the ten-second countdown began they added it to their cart with ease and confidence.

I also enhanced this program by making all customers, from the first moment they purchase, default "members" with a 10 percent discount for life on any new collection. The only marketing material they received for the program was a summary of their purchases throughout the year, and the requirements to become a ten-second owner.

No email registration. No inbox full of promotions.

Now imagine yourself as the owner of a fashion boutique. A customer walks up to the register to make a purchase. You tell her everything I just described to you about the ten-second owner program. Your customer looks at you amazed.

"Are you serious? I can do all that without giving you my email?"

You smile and assure them that yes, that is correct.

Owing to this program, the boutiques I managed were able to collect an incredible amount of mouse-to-mouse data, increase their loyal customer base by 40 percent, and see a 30 percent increase in revenue—all in less than three months.

The ten-second owner program was a Happening that enabled customers to make their own magic every 365 days.

Providing every customer this sense of ownership encourages them to become ambassadors for your brand and helps you to further differentiate your brand from competitors. And creating a sense of ownership within a customer base is possible, no matter your industry.

Take time to talk with each one of your associates about enhancing your loyalty program, and then present it to customers in a way that entices them.

Ask your associates:

- Why will customers want to join?
- What will keep them coming back?
- What is the value they receive?
- How can we bring them into this program without adding work or effort?
- How can we bring this into our daily services?

Another example is a simple points system. Add 25 loyalty points to a customer's account for every $100 spent, equal to $25 to redeem. Make sure to display the points on the price tag of your product or service, so that customers can see what their points are able to purchase. Then, customers will join willingly because they know that spending $400 will earn them an extra $100 in additional products or services.

Of course, you can adjust the numbers to what you offer, but by placing the point system right beside the products and services customers are about to purchase, you keep the experience of shopping with you interesting and pointing toward future rewards. And this program can be automated.

Bold Action and Execution

In addition to reaching customers at the soul level and offering them a sense of ownership, you must be bold. Happenings you create as a result of executing bold actions will have a greater impact on your customers.

During the summer of 2017, my mother and sister spent a few weeks in Zaragoza, Spain, visiting my aunt and uncle. At that time I was working in Jamaica and hadn't seen my mother or uncle in over two years. So when I found out that my family would be in Spain, I booked a flight to Madrid on a mission expressly to create a Happening.

After landing in Madrid, I did some investigating to find out where they would be having lunch that Sunday. Then, early that morning, I took a train into Zaragoza and arrived at the restaurant just as my family members were ordering drinks and food.

Without being seen, I explained the Happening I had planned to the restaurant manager.

"I need your help to surprise my family."

"Certainly, sir," said the manager.

"In the back, there is a big table full of noisy people. You know the one I mean?"

The manager laughed and nodded.

"That's them. I haven't seen them for a long time. I want to do something to make them uncomfortable for a few minutes, and then transform that into joy."

The manager understood immediately what I meant by that. And I believe that he was more excited than me to see my family's reaction.

So he helped me prepare for my little performance. I put on a staff apron and cap, and picked up the bottle of wine that my Uncle Charbel had ordered. I went to the table and allowed Charbel to taste the first sip.

Neither he nor anyone in my family noticed that it was me, probably because I'd pulled the cap so low on my face and because I'd grown a beard since the last time they saw me.

Charbel took a sip, then turned to me and said, "Outstanding wine."

"Okay," I replied, disguising my voice, "let's see if this wine is as good as you say."

I then served myself a glass and drank it in one gulp, like it was a shot of tequila.

Now, my uncle is a formal person who gets upset quite quickly when people do things without manners or decorum. As soon as I swallowed the wine, his face turned red, then green, then yellow, and every other color.

"*Please*," he said, raising his voice, "take this bottle away and bring us another one, and then you can finish the rest of the bottle yourself."

"Wow," I said with a soft, polite voice of sincere gratitude. "Thank you so much for offering me this bottle. And yes, it is a great wine. I'll leave it here so that my manager does not get upset with me, and will immediately open another one for you."

Before going back to fetch another bottle, I served myself another glass, raised it in the air while saying "Cheers," and gulped it down like it was another shot. I left the bottle on the table and left.

As I walked away, I could hear everyone at the table laughing. Then I heard a chair skid across the floor. Without looking back, I knew it was my uncle, getting up from the table, most likely very upset. Two seconds later he brushed past me and marched right up to the manager to let him know all the reasons why his waiter was a piece of garbage.

Meanwhile, I still had several more elements of my Happening to execute, so I quickly and quietly scooted back to the table, sat in his place, and served myself another glass of wine.

One by one, the faces around me changed from bewilderment to recognition as they realized it was me the whole time. Everyone came over to hug and kiss me.

"My son! My son!" my mother exclaimed. "My son, this is the best day of my life. Now my holidays have officially begun!"

On the other side of the restaurant, Charbel saw his family members, including his wife, hugging this strange waiter. I could feel his fury as he stomped back over the table, fully prepared to act as a family defender and put this random waiter in his place. Before he could read me the riot act, I immediately took off the cap. My uncle saw my face and could hardly believe it. He was so happy and relieved that he didn't have to upbraid anyone that he started laughing.

"That was above and beyond any surprise," he said. He then hugged me and shouted, "You can pay for the wine!"

For this *Happening*, I went beyond surprising my family and took bold action to provide an out-of-the-box reunion experience for the people I love.

Though this may appear to be just a funny anecdote, there is a lesson to be learned here that can be applied to the way you do business.

First, I share this story to show you the difference between merely surprising people and using bold energy and a daring attitude to create Happenings. No matter your industry, you need to push the boundaries of what your customers expect. Provide over-the-top and out-of-the-box experiences. Seek new ways to provoke extraordinary feelings in your customers.

Empower your team to build Happening moments, based on bold ideas. For example, if you're selling a physical product, like cosmetics or perfume, have your associates package up a few samples, away from the customer's line of vision, and write a note, "I hope you enjoy these. Here is my # ---- where you can contact me with any questions. I look forward to your return." Then, when your customer makes the purchase, wrap up the samples with the product, along with the note—and don't say anything about the samples.

When the customer gets home and opens the package, she will find those small details that are normally given away casually, without making a connection or creating the experience of surprise. With this simple gesture, you will create a Happening for your customer.

The "Wow" Factor

In 2016, I traveled to Japan to deliver a keynote to hospitality industry leaders on how to enhance the customer experience. Four weeks before the trip, the convention host sent me a fifteen-second introduction video.

"Hello, my name is Katsumi. I am your host for the upcoming event. I am looking forward to meeting you in person and anxiously await your arrival. Your driver, Kristi, will pick you up from the airport. He is fluent in English and will offer you a tour of the city before the convention starts. Please let me know if you have any questions. If you have time this week, I would love to have a phone call with you, at your convenience, to discuss details. Have a wonderful day."

I hadn't even arrived yet and the convention organizers were already making an emotional connection with me. The words *anxiously await, tour of the city,* and *at your convenience* told me how much she was dedicated to the success of my arrival!

Have you ever received a video like this from an event host? Probably not. The truth is very few hosts actually connect with customers before they arrive. At best, the hotel sends you a link to an app you're supposed to download or a pre-arrival form you're supposed to fill out. Chances are you do neither of these things, because who has the time?

And my phone call with Katsumi was even more impressive.

"Hello, this is Katsumi, your host for the convention in Japan. Am I speaking to Mr. Johnny?"

"Hello, Katsumi, yes indeed. Please, call me Johnny."

"It's a pleasure to speak with you, Johnny. We are very much looking forward to welcoming you to our country, and learning from you at the convention. We have confirmed three thousand attendees, isn't that exciting?"

I was quite wowed with that number, and told her so.

"I have sent you the program, and wanted to quickly recap before your arrival so all you need to know is when to be there, and you won't have to worry about any of the other details. Are you okay doing the opening talk?"

"Yes, I am honored to. Thank you, Katsumi."

"Do you have any special requests or concerns as far as the technical part goes?"

"Not at the moment. The chart you sent me is perfect."

She told me that I was welcome to rehearse before the convention if I felt I needed to, and that she would adapt my presentation to their system if I sent it to her beforehand. She explained that I would have a monitor in front of me if needed as well as a time frame so I could adjust my timing. Also, upon the arrival to my hotel room I would be provided with a tablet on which I could see the order of my presentation and the content. If I had any changes I could make them directly on the tablet and they would go directly to the main system.

Katsumi continued going through all the details, making sure that no mistake could be made. She was looking to ensure my comfort, and to make sure that I would feel confident and stress-free before the convention. I ended that phone call with an incredible sense of ease and trust that all would go well.

The date of the convention arrived and after thirty hours in flight, my driver, Kristi, was waiting for me at the airport exit, just as Katsumi had promised. He offered me my favorite drink upon getting into the car, as well as wet towels to refresh my face, and photos of the hotel—amazing after the long-haul travel.

"Would you like the tour?" he asked me.

"I'm very tired," I replied, "so I prefer to go straight to the hotel. But on the way, can you give me a few highlights of the city?"

Kristi agreed and took me straight to the hotel, in contact with Katsumi via live screen the whole way. Katsumi greeted me right in the lobby, just as she promised, by which time I felt like I'd known her for a long, long time. She escorted me to my room, where I completed the check in. Already, my arrival was a success, but little did I know there was more in store.

"Johnny," said Katsumi, gesturing toward a man the size of a Sumo wrestler, "this is Maku."

I smiled.

"Maku is going to apply 10m pressure to your back to help you sleep better, okay?"

"Absolutely," I said aloud. Inwardly, I was thinking, OMG, this man is a mountain. A little bit of pressure from him and I'll not only sleep better, I'll sleep *forever*.

Yet with the grace of a ballerina, Maku picked me up by the back of my trousers, raised me into the air and then placed me down on a wooden table. Maku started speaking to me in Japanese and pulling on my shirt. Was he giving me orders? Insulting my body or my choice of clothing? Finally, I understood that he wanted me to take off my shirt and lie down, which I did.

He then put his massive hands on my back and started applying pressure. It felt like a big truck was rolling over me. Like the cartoon in which the roadrunner is always running from the coyote who gets smashed with a car or a truck.

Yet, no more than fifteen minutes later I felt a strong desire to crawl into bed and never come out. Normally, I struggle to sleep the night before a big presentation, but after the truck (aka Maku) rolled along my back, I slept like a baby. I've never slept so peacefully before an event in my life.

Wow. I enjoyed the most amazing arrival, and sleep support. The trip was already a success in my book. But there was more.

The next day, I was backstage preparing for my keynote speech. Katsumi guided me to a corner and offered me sparkling water. As I took a sip, Katsumi held out a tablet for me to see. On the screen was a recorded message from my wife and daughter wishing me the best for the convention.

"Johnny, we are so proud of you! We cannot be present in the room but we are with you all the time, as Katsumi is live streaming your speech for us. We will be watching and sending you lots of love and positive energy."

My daughter barely pronounces words. But she said, "Papa you," which means "I love you."

Katsumi, in addition to everything else she did, was sure to communicate with my wife and ask her for this favor. And believe me, that message generated a wealth of energy and positive emotions.

A few seconds later, Maku appeared, smiling.

"Oh, no!" I laughed, unsure of what to expect. He picked me up like a doll, again, crunched my back, and then set my feet back down on the floor. I felt like a new person.

The time eventually came for me to deliver my presentation. It was supposed to be forty-five minutes long, and I chose to invest ten minutes of that time sharing my experience with Katsumi and the Happenings that she made possible.

Then, as other speakers delivered their presentations, they each mentioned Katsumi and the experiences she created for them as well. This was in front of more than three thousand attendees, and after each speech they all stood on their feet and gave us thunderous applause.

Katsumi didn't have to spend a dime marketing herself or her company because of the energy and enjoyment she created around each speaker.

The "wow" can be generated in any business, with any brand, offering any product or service through a simple yet steadfast commitment to communicating effectively. Here's what I mean by that:

- **Find something in common with your customer.** Share with enthusiasm. This helps you calibrate your language to the language of the customer.
- **Don't assume or deduce what you think the customer wants.** Most times they don't know what they want and need you to figure it out and offer them what they could never anticipate beforehand.
- **Always take the opportunity to ask the customer questions that will give you crucial insight on what is important to them.** Does your customer need a cup of coffee fast, and to go, to get to the airport on time? Does your customer want to find a one-of-a-kind gift for a special occasion? And so on.

- **Communicate your findings to every member of your team who will be at each touchpoint of that customer's interaction with your brand.** Make sure everyone is ready to move mountains to get that customer checked out on the way to the airport, rather than having to do it on property. Have everyone search your inventory high and low for special gifts that your customer can take home.

- **Look at what's invisible to the customer.** Create an experience that solves their problems and makes their day better, something they will never anticipate on their own. You have all the tools at hand to surprise with how you can offer service.

Know your customer, and transmit this to your team. Commit to this first, and do it for each customer without fail, and the revenue will follow.

A Sense of Mystery and Surprise

In the summer of 2006, I took my wife, Vanessa, to Bangkok to celebrate our wedding anniversary. On one of the nights we celebrated with dinner at a traditional Thai restaurant by the riverside. As the hostess led us to our table, she carried on a simple conversation with us.

"How do you find our country?" she asked.

"We love it. Thank you."

"What do you love about it?"

"It's the people that make the experience here so great, though we also love the temples, history, and authenticity as well."

As the light questions continued we let her know that we were there to celebrate our wedding anniversary, and that the concierge at our hotel had recommended that restaurant. Vanessa and I thought nothing more of this exchange and sat down to order. Yet, just by asking these simple questions, our hostess had learned that this particular evening meant a great deal to us.

Within minutes, the first courses of a delicious meal had arrived. And as expected, it was delicious. Thai dancers entered the room to perform a traditional dance as more dishes were served, set to the background of a stunning view of the river and city skyline. This was turning out to be the "wow" celebration that we had hoped for on our special day.

This was the restaurant's standard service, and little did we know that they had something special up their sleeve just for us.

The hostess approached as my wife and I finished our meal and informed us that a dessert was being prepared in our honor, and that if we would please follow her they would serve it to us at a different location. We hadn't ordered a dessert—the restaurant had taken it upon themselves to treat us because we had chosen them to celebrate our anniversary. As this was all unfolding I looked at Vanessa, who was beaming. We felt like celebrities.

Our hostess asked us to follow her, but wouldn't tell us where we were going. She led us to the back of the restaurant, which was quite dark and even a little scary, which added to the sense of mystery. Suddenly, she stopped, and told us that she could not go further, but if we used the flashlight and took another ten or steps forward we would come to a bridge. There would be a man waiting for us there, whom we would need to give a password—Khwām rak—to continue. She told us that he would take care of everything from that point onward.

We had no idea what that password meant, and weren't entirely sure how we would get back to the main part of the restaurant, but we decided to go along with it. We found the man on the bridge, and gave him the password, and he led us to our surprise.

A small boat was floating in the river, waiting for us. As we got closer we could see that it was filled with flowers and candles. We were told that it belonged to us for the evening, and to please enjoy it for as long as we liked. Amazing!

Once we stepped into the boat and settled ourselves, we noticed both a waiter and a chef on the shoreline. The waiter held a tray, on which I could see candles and tiny desserts. By that time, Vanessa and I had already drifted out a few feet. There was no way the waiter could hand us the tray without dropping all those candles into the water. Without hesitating, the waiter stepped into the water. Holding the tray carefully, he waded out to our boat and handed us the tray. On the bank, the chef told us about each dessert—all the ingredients and how they were made. Wow!

The waiter told us that the password—Khwām rak—was Thai for love. And then they both wished us a happy anniversary and left us alone.

Vanessa and I stayed for two hours, enjoying the candles and desserts, an entire bottle of champagne and other drinks. The boat experience was so full of magic and beauty it will never be forgotten, and will always be held as a most cherished memory.

It wasn't until later that I realized it was a direct result of our hostess and those simple questions she asked us when she was leading us to our table. What I thought was just small talk turned into an opportunity for her to rally the staff around celebrating our anniversary. The best part was the sense of mystery around each new phase of the evening. Vanessa and I had so much fun anticipating what was next, we never felt afraid of the unexpected.

I love the idea of creating a mysterious experience for the customer. Mystery is powerful and attractive—we as humans want to know what's going on and what's going to happen. Your customer wants to experience a sense of mystery. This is why clandestine entry points you have to be in the know to access, and provide a password for, are so popular. The same goes for blind dinners or even bar experiences, during which guests are blindfolded or in a pitch-black room and have to guess the ingredients of each dish or drink. Some even use this blind menu concept as a "test" for diners, and only if they can guess correctly are they invited to a special dinner.

Even Capital One has capitalized on a sense of mystery and surprise with their Capital One Cafés. The bank doubles as a coffee shop that provides conference rooms for free, happy hours for customers with a Capital One card, free activities such as yoga, and giveaways for special occasions. Every day there is something new to both surprise and delight the customer.

Creating Story-Worthy Experiences

Give your customers experiences that they can tell a story about over and over again.

One of the best stories I have, though quite unintentionally created, centered around my wedding day. It was August 29, 2002, the day before the marriage ceremony, and we were holding the rehearsal at the Carthusian Monastery in Spain. The wedding was taking place in a village called Valldemossa, in Mallorca, where my wife is from.

Valldemossa is one of the most picturesque villages in Mallorca. It's a charming town that has been able to preserve the style and ambiance of centuries past, and maintain its rich cultural heritage. Santa Catalina Thomas was born in Valldemossa in 1533, and visitors are able to admire small tiles with prayers or drawings of her next to the door of almost every home in the village. Polish composer Frédéric Chopin and French writer George Sand both lived at the monastery, and made the village famous.

The public is not allowed to be married at the Carthusian Monastery, though we were able to get permission granted from the patriarch based on my future wife's family history. Vanessa's grandfather founded the traditional dance of Valldemossa, and her father is related to a famous band from the village whose popularity helped promote the island of Mallorca as a destination and boost its tourism trade. To this day, each Sunday families and musicians—including my then future father-in-law—gather at the village church and offer song and dance to Santa Catalina.

But on the day of the rehearsal, I decided to go to the nearby city of Palma. I had until 5:00 in the evening on my own to do some shopping before the festivities began. Days are quite long during the summer in Mallorca, especially in August when you can still enjoy daylight as late as 10:00 at night. With two hours to go before the rehearsal, I stopped at a café to read a newspaper and have a bite to eat. The café was near where the rehearsal was taking place, so I thought it would be a good place to pass the time.

Now, I am a punctual person. I am always on time, and if I happen to be late, it is generally safe to assume that something is wrong. So when my future brother-in-law approached me after I'd been at the café about an hour and a half, I thought nothing of it. He asked if I was ready for tomorrow, I told him I was, and that I was going to be heading to the rehearsal at the monastery shortly. He asked when it would be, to which I replied 5:00 p.m. He said he wouldn't be able to join, but he would see me at the dinner later and wished me luck.

I was keeping an eye on my watch, and at 4:55 I began the walk up the hill to the church for the rehearsal. I saw that Malen, Vanessa's aunt, was standing at the entrance waiting for me.

"Hi, Malen, how are you?"

She replied with a slap to my face, and then quickly asked me if I was alright.

"How can I be alright if you just slapped me?"

"We thought you had an accident," she explained, knowing that the road between Valldemossa and Palma hugs a cliff, and hugged me in relief. She then informed me that I was two hours late.

It was 7:00, not 5:00, like I'd thought. My watch had apparently broken and I had been none the wiser until I received that slap in face. Everyone was waiting for me, worried that something had gone wrong.

Vanessa ran up to me, relieved that I was fine and hugging me tightly. She told me that they'd had all the friends and family, the police, and even the fire station out looking for me. Basically they'd moved the entire village to find out what had happened. I was astounded, and effusively apologetic.

When we finally made it into the church—two hours after we were supposed to start—the priest looked at me and shook his head.

"Johnny, Johnny, Johnny," he said, with another slap to my face. "I hope you are on time tomorrow!" The look on his face brooked no argument.

So, this was now twice in total that I was slapped in the face before getting married. I knew that I had no way out of the wedding in this tightly knit village with all my soon-to-be wife's family around, even if I wanted one, which I emphatically did not.

The funny thing is, to this day no one believes me that I was a mere 200 meters away from the church, and that my broken watch was the real culprit for why I was so late. They call it the "uncertain rehearsal," joking that I wasn't sure whether to run away or not. Some still ask me what really happened, convinced that there must be some other version of the real truth. It doesn't help that my brother-in-law can't remember what time he passed me at the cafe, so I have no help from that quarter.

When the time came to marry Vanessa that next day, you can bet I was on time. All the attendees clapped when I entered the church, including members of my own family. The joke was on me due to the events of the previous day, and this crazy, unexpected scenario created a Happening—a story-worthy experience—that our family, friends, and even the villagers still remember.

Why do I share this personal story about my own wedding? Two reasons, mainly. The first, to illustrate the value of time.

Clients value their time above all else. In today's consumer culture, customers want to have everything quickly, with as little wait time as possible. They are willing to pay more to shorten that wait time even a little bit. I have a reputation for being punctual and professional, which has served me well in my career since it is known that I respect my clients' time, and they in turn respect mine.

I understand as well that humans crave social interaction. It is essential to know how to manage your clients' time when they are interacting with your business, and operate with a high level of professionalism when it comes to the timeliness of a delivery or response.

This respect of others' time nurtures relationships and allows trust to grow. If you can answer the needs and demands of your customers, and solve any problems quickly and efficiently, your business will increase in esteem in their eyes. Be on time for your customers, and your team. Show them the professionalism and respect you have for them. Use time to help you create Happenings.

The second reason I shared my rehearsal story is to emphasize the part we each play in a story itself.

Why do we rehearse for weddings? We all have a basic idea of what's supposed to happen, so why do we have to practice beforehand? Consider this though: the bride and the groom are the main actors on this special day. Actors and actresses have countless rehearsals in order to ensure perfection for the big performance. So why leave a day as important as a wedding to chance?

Your customers are the protagonists of the story—the Happening—that you create and personalize for them. You are tasked with designing a rehearsal for your team to ensure a perfect delivery of a story-worthy experience, one that will create the impact and evoke the emotions that guarantee that it will never be forgotten, and often relived through retelling.

Be deliberate in your choice of Happening to design for your guests, and the exact scene you want to create. Decide the location and rehearse it. Try to see it through the eyes of the guest who will shortly live it. Is it functional, or is it emotional? If it's emotional, you're on the track. Choose something enjoyable, and have fun creating it.

Questions

Following are three practices that will help you perform in a way that wows your customer at every touchpoint.

First Practice: Write Your Script

What do you have to do to make the desire of your customer come true? What you have to do to transform the desire into impact. What can be impactful for you? It might be nothing for your customer. How do you make sure that your performance is going to have an emotional impact on your customer?

Write down the desire that your customer already gave you. Think about how you can create an emotional impact around those desires to increase the level of loyalty and make the difference.

For example, if your customer wants to feel important and valued, you can make sure that your staff learns their names, communicates their names between peers, and shares the customer's habits and demands, such as their favorite drink or whether they are celebrating anything.

Communication between peers will help your peers make the customer feel special and you will create an emotional impact on them. For example, if you know that your customer is vegetarian, surprise them by telling them you have had a vegetarian menu sent to their room, and that the waiter at the bar knows and has ordered a vegetable plate to complement their drink. Communication is key to create those emotional impact.

Ask your customer about moments that they lived at your establishment or other places and learn from it. For example, if you learn that your customer enjoyed the landscaping of your resort, send them a picture of the grounds with descriptions of the variety of plants and how they take care of them.

Describe the emotional impact of a personal or professional experience you have had.

Now think how you could adapt those memories to the desire of your customers.

For example, one day after we had gone shopping, my daughter left her iPad in the parking lot, but we didn't realize it until three hours later. I drove twenty minutes back to the parking lot and asked the security guard if she had found it. The answer was no, but that didn't mean we couldn't find it.

The security guard's demeanor surprised me, as security guards are usually a bit stiff. We went together to the parking space that I remembered. As we walked, I thought about how a person's attitude and small gestures can have an impact on you. Luckily for me the iPad was there. I was happy to find it, of course, but the guard's equal excitement that we found it was memorable. I can still hear her laugh in my ears.

Share the answers with your team and peers to increase the sense of creating those emotional impacts. Build an emotional impacts panel or internal channel where everyone can share their stories and the emotional impacts they make or receive.

Second Practice: Direct Yourself Backstage

Work with the human resources department to create emotional impact for your associates. That will help your associates understand the meaning and the how. For example, build a guest experience scene board where employees can design scenes—visual representations of the exact experiences they want customers to have, down to every single detail.

Imagine when your customer enters your store or your office, how they behave.

Do they look to the right or left? If they look to the right, then make sure that you place on the right side something that makes them think *I love this place* as they walk in and out. It can be some word of welcome them, maybe yourself greeting them, maybe a drink with a message *I was waiting for you.* You need images of every single one of these details so that your team can see them and memorize the scene.

For example, pick up a magazine that goes with your brand look and feel. Start by cutting images of how you want that experience to be delivered, why you chose this particular experience, when you are going to deliver it, who is going to do it, and how you are going to measure that the experience delivered was assertive, and whether the experience made a positive impact on your customer. Finally classify use stars to indicate how successful the experience was.

Base this on the profile of your customer. By imagining and sharing on your GEX scene board, your team members will enjoy sharing and enriching your idea, learning from it and preparing to deliver it. If you are able to create a GEX app, it could connect to human resources, where they can detect the percentage of happy associates, and send positive messages and offers of help to those who are not feeling well.

Third Practice: Close the Curtain

Now that you have a clear picture of your new role as a leader, create an action plan. What will you do differently to create an emotional impact? When you will do it? Where you will do it?

Next, evaluate your success. How does this emotional impact make customers behave differently? Are they more loyal? Are you having more positive feedback? Are you having more employees named on social media or service evaluation forms? How does your team embrace the idea of becoming more aware of the emotional impact?

Now celebrate with your team what you were able to achieve together. Reward the team for the emotional impact made for your customer. Employee rewards must be personalized if at all possible—the secret is to build an assortment that everyone will be excited to earn. The rewards can be loyalty points that they can redeem for a hotel stay or store purchase, or you can use these ideas:

- Spotify Premium or Apple Music subscription
- Plants
- Gift cards
- Rented or professionally styled outfits for special occasions
- Personal recognition note from CEO
- Laundry ticket
- Motivational ebook
- Online course subscription
- Dinner for two
- Museum tickets
- Zoo tickets for the family
- Books
- Massage
- Facial exfoliation
- Wellness coach
- Babysitter for one night
- New office chair
- Photo shoot to "be a model for a day"
- Mani/pedi
- Financial consultant session
- Growth consultant session
- Cooking class
- Music lesson
- Drawing lesson
- Yoga lesson
- Personal trainer voucher
- Car wash
- Full tank of gas

All the above perks build rapport.

Cultivate a culture so contagious that your internal customers can't help but master it, live it, and transmit it to others every day.

7

Burst through Your Hesitation

In 2016, my company, JSK MIND, felt like it was moving forward in slow motion. The business was suffering from a cash flow problem. The reason for this problem, however, wasn't disorganized books, massive debts, or issues with profit —it had to do with the payment policies. Late payments were an issue, particularly from larger companies.

I knew that in order to generate more income, I needed to expand my market. I was already working toward creating more brand recognition and generating new leads by offering free conferences at hotels owned by big companies. During these events I delivered a two-and-a-half-hour talk on enhancing customer experience and trends in the market, which competencies associates need in order to take service from good to great, and insights on creating the wow factor. The talk had a workshop element, during which participants interacted and learned through experience, with the objective being for attendees to see firsthand my know-how in customer experience and training skills.

As rewarding as these conferences were for everyone involved, I really needed to move my company forward! I knew that consistently giving my best to small companies would eventually open the doors to working with larger companies. I also knew that it was time to start closing those big corporate deals.

My vision for JSK MIND was to create world-class leaders in the hospitality industry, who inspire current and future generations through meaningful, lasting opportunities. We would do this by building better learning by experience practices, both offline and online, that would help our culture thrive and succeed. But if I didn't do something fast, this vision I had so carefully created would be in serious danger of fizzling out.

So what to do? I considered my options: investing, traveling, giving more free conferences. Perhaps I should refine my marketing strategy, or wait patiently for some new opportunity to present itself. What kind of opportunity was I even looking for? And how would I know I was doing the right thing and not just spinning my wheels, and when would I know? Did I even need to be worried about growth?

In this chapter, I am going to teach you how to transform challenges into opportunity. First, let me tell you a story.

One day, the phone rang. It was Cecile Rivals, the human resources director of Sol Group America. I have known Cecile since 1996, when we met at a seminar in Cuba. At this time, I was working for Meliá Hotels International, as the entertainment and customer service director for the Dominican Republic and Mexico. We saw each other ten years later at another seminar in Spain, and then at a party in Miami in 2016, the year of my struggles.

Cecile and I have always had a great relationship. She and my wife, Vanessa, worked in the same corporate office in Miami, though in different departments. It was Vanessa who gave me the heads up that Cecile had asked for my phone number, and might be calling. No other details were shared with me.

Naturally, my brain started turning. Cecile might be calling me for something big. I was getting excited, thinking about the possibilities.

And then, the phone rang.

"Johnny, I have a challenge for you that I think you'll enjoy," she said, and then she paused, awaiting my reaction.

As soon as I heard the word *challenge*, I thought for sure it must be a *real* challenge. I was familiar with her team, and how skillful they are, and I knew the companies she usually used for consulting, and they were extremely competent companies. So what does she mean by *challenge*?

Perhaps it was a challenge for her and her team, and for me it would be a chance for growth, stability, and transformation. If so, then my mission would be to help Cecile and her team see that I had the ability to turn that challenge into an opportunity. Or maybe they were looking at this challenge through a certain lens, and it would be my chance to step in with a different perspective, and present fresh, new possibilities. What I knew for sure, though, was that I needed to come up with whatever solution they needed in such a way that they would be able to visualize a positive outcome—one in which the challenge disappeared.

"What's the challenge?" I asked Cecile.

"It's designing a personalized project that mixes diversity training with customer experience training, in the form of a workshop for all the company's hotels based in North and South America."

I couldn't believe what I was hearing. This was exactly the sort of project I needed in order to keep my own company afloat and save it from the slow-motion gap. A significant opportunity like this could keep my vision alive, and I loved that Cecile reached out to me with this challenge.

"You will be competing with three other companies," she continued.

"How so?"

"These other companies have already presented their ideas for the project, and one of them is standing out as quite strong and competitive."

I had worked with Meliá Hotels International for twenty years at this point, so I felt confident to face this challenge and my competition. Meliá was founded in 1956 in Palma de Mallorca, Spain, and is the largest hotel chain in Spain in both resort and city hotels. It is also one of the largest hotel companies in the world, currently operating more than 370 hotels in 43 countries and four continents under its brand names: Meliá, Gran Meliá, ME by Meliá, Paradisus, Innside by Meliá, TRYP by Wyndham, Sol Beach House Hotels and Circle.

"As you know," Cecile continued, "we have been working globally with a company for more than twenty years, but we believe that your know-how in customer experience might bring something new and unexpected."

Twenty years is a rare kind of loyalty in any industry. I was flattered to be approached, and quite frankly a little speechless.

"Well, thank you, I'm…"

"And Johnny?" she interjected when I paused. "I am betting on you."

"Really?"

"Absolutely. We need your creativity, and I have no doubt that you'll do something different. Are you willing to take that bet?"

"Of course! I appreciate the opportunity, and I'm in 100 percent!"

It was at this instant that I knew I had the perfect opportunity—the exact project I'd been hoping and dreaming and praying for. I was in the exact right place at the right time, and I could hardly believe my divine luck.

The one catch? Cecile was traveling to Spain one week from that day to present the project, and I'd need to have my draft ready to present when she returned.

That was a short time! Would I be able to come up with an idea that would be a hit so quickly? I could feel the stress start to creep in, and I found myself hesitating. I was well aware that although Cecile gave me until she returned from Spain to present my idea, my best chances of securing the project would be to have it ready beforehand.

If I hesitated too long, and let the fear plant doubts in my mind, I would lose this opportunity. A split second later I knew what I was going to do.

"I can have it ready for you before you travel."

"How about the end of this week?" she asked.

I pulled up my calendar. There were only four days left that week, which meant I had little to no time to learn what she meant by mixing diversity culture with customer experience, much less to develop a memorable and engaging workshop experience. Despite the short turnaround time, my instinct was telling me, *Johnny, there is only one right answer here. Don't hesitate any longer.*

"Yes," I said, the very next second.

Cecile was delighted, and began describing the project. I would be tasked with creating a training experience that would encourage associates to embrace cultural differences and become enthusiastic, committed, creative, energized contributors to the international essence of the company by highlighting diversity and integrating with local culture. And, she informed me, the pilot workshop would be for the pre-opening of Meliá Jamaica, Montego Bay.

Now I understood the challenge. It wasn't just the workshop content—it was also the territory chosen to kick off this training. This was a deliberate choice on her part. Jamaica poses a multitude of barriers for a European company, from culture differentiation, leadership mindset, conceptualization, delivery of service, novelty of customer experience, and so on. If you can overcome these and be successful in Jamaica, you can be successful in any other country in the Americas. It was the perfect place to test this pilot program.

I was getting more and more excited, and one idea after another started popping up in my mind. I only had four days to put something together, but I knew right then and there that this project belonged to me. And the more I thought about it, the more I realized that I had nothing to lose, and everything to gain. If I put every ounce of my energy and creativity into this proposal, I could create something that would blow everyone's mind.

As soon as I hung up with Cecile, I started Googling. I was searching for information on diversity culture that could give me a starting point. I even went to the library to find more resources for further investigation. I was so inspired by the topic that I spent the whole night brainstorming a design for the project.

After hours of being in this creative energy, an idea was starting to take shape. I knew firsthand what it was like to be a foreigner, living in various countries. Anywhere I've either lived or traveled has always presented the question of how to make people see me as the person I am, rather than an outsider. I've had to overcome this challenge in both day-to-day life and in the workplace, and through those experiences learned a great deal about the meaning of and value behind diversity culture.

In order to thrive as a foreigner, you must adapt your beliefs and values to accommodate those of the country you're in. This doesn't mean you have to throw who you are out the window— just learn to approach every encounter with an open mind. Be empathetic, and patient. Don't lose your temper because they don't do things your way, or because someone made some offhand comment about you. Some people may even want you to fail, because of where you're from. It has nothing to do with who you actually are.

This connection I made between my own experience as a foreigner and the focus on diversity with Cecile's project brought a story to mind, which I will share with you now.

I had applied for a job once, with the interview process conducted entirely via telephone. The woman interviewing me was super friendly and efficient, all around an amazing communicator, and at the end of the hour conversation she offered me the job. She welcomed me to the "family" and said that in two days she'd follow up with me to go through the details. I was thrilled, and very much looking forward to meeting her personally after such a positive interview experience.

The next day, I received a phone call from the director of human resources.

"Is this Mr. Johnny Sfeir?"

"Yes, this is Johnny. What can I do for you?"

"Unfortunately, I called to inform you that my colleague made a mistake in offering you the position yesterday. We cannot bring you on board as all the candidates have already been selected."

"Strange," I replied, "because your colleague told me that she still needed at least thirty candidates to fill the available slots, and even asked me to connect her with anyone I know who has a similar profile and language skills as mine."

"Well, the issue is that you don't have the competencies we're looking for," he tried to explain.

It was then that I realized what he was actually trying to do was convince me of a reason—any reason—as to why I wasn't a fit for the job, without telling me the truth of the matter.

I told him, with respect, he and I both knew that I had exactly what they were looking for in a candidate, and asked him to tell me exactly what the problem was or the competencies missing so that I could work on them. I expressed my interest in working for the company, so I was willing to fix whatever these issues were.

To my shock, if not surprise, the director of human resources replied to me that the reason was because I am *moro*, and the company doesn't hire *moros*. In Spanish, *moro* is a slang word referring to Arabic Muslims from the regions of Maghreb, Morocco, Algeria, Tunisia, Libya, and Mauritania. It's a racist word at worst, stereotyping at best.

"With all my respect to *moros*, I am actually not one. But so what if I was? Why don't you hire *moros*?" I asked. "I've been a resident of this country for more than six years, pay taxes like any citizen, and never disrespect any nationality or religion."

I then asked him if his company offered services to foreigners, to which he replied yes, they do. So I asked him, how are they able to do this if they disrespect races? He told me that it wasn't my problem and swiftly hung up the phone.

I ended that call pretty frustrated and upset, understandably. I was upset enough to reach out to my Uncle Sami to share this awful experience. I knew he had a close friend involved with the company somehow, so I thought he would be the right person to offer insight and guidance.

My uncle assured me that they must not be aware of such behavior. He described the owners as respectful, warm people and lamented the shame of having human resources directors such as the one I spoke with who comport themselves in a manner which reflects poorly on a company of prestige.

My uncle told me to call back and speak to the person who originally interviewed me, and ask her if she agreed with the argument put forth by the human resources director. If she answered yes, then he advised me to move on and have nothing more to do with the situation. But if her answer was no, then he would help me land this opportunity.

I considered his advice for a moment, and then told him I didn't want to harm anyone, and maybe it just wasn't meant to be. He encouraged me to at least call my interviewer, and see if she was in fact aware of the situation and the reason for my rejection, and to thank her for her time. No need for judgment, criticism, or drama.

I called my interviewer. She answered on the second ring.

"Oh, Johnny, I heard about the cancellation of your position here," she said, "and if you're calling me to ask whether or not I believe you're able to do the job then my answer is yes, you absolutely are."

She went on to say that she did not agree with the human resources director in regard to the *moros* argument, and that she was totally against that argument and felt it went against the company's policy. She also explained with the regret that there was nothing she could do about it. She promised that if anyone asked her about my abilities and whether or not the company needed someone of my skills, she would definitely recommend me and go to bat for me. I was floored by her sincerity, and beyond grateful for her support.

That same day, my uncle put his wheels in motion by contacting a friend who is a cousin to the company's CEO. This friend couldn't believe what she was hearing as my uncle told my tale, and promised to call her cousin immediately. But this wasn't the sort of favor my uncle was currying—rather, he asked for a recommendation if he faxed over my CV.

Two days later, I had a telegram from that same human resources director. At this time formal offers were sent either by fax, telex, or telegram, so I had an idea of what it said.

It read, "Congratulations, Mr. Sfeir. You have been selected to be part of our family. Please get in touch with … for all the details. We will see you soon."

When I arrived at the office on my first day, I was approached by this now infamous human resources director.

"You are very well connected," he said, "why didn't you start there versus going through an interview process?"

"I wanted to do things correctly, without special favors," I replied.

He told me that I gave him an important lesson, and that he owed me an apology. I asked him, "What lesson could I have given you?"

"You didn't mention the words that were said when I spoke with you to your connections here. That says a lot about who you are, and how you face things. It's a lesson for me to think differently about foreigners."

He asked me why I never mentioned to my contacts within the company that he called me a *moro*. I told him that I had to be smart, otherwise he'd make my life miserable should I end up being hired. He laughed, and requested that we start over. It was my wish as well, so I readily agreed.

Within six months this human resources director was assigning me initiatives that included traveling throughout Spain and Europe with his team, as part of a task force seeking new candidates to hire. I became part of his circle of trust, and his diversity differentiation altered completely in an overwhelmingly positive way.

By revisiting this experience, I began to remember other experiences, and all the details that go into adapting one's lifestyle to fit with different countries. All the cultures I was exposed to, the traditions and values I absorbed, and the people and food I encountered taught me about crossing barriers and learning to not only survive, but thrive in each new situation.

It was through these experiences that I was able to create a simulation workshop during which participants could not only experience, but also enjoy their time, and live diversity in every interaction. I was able to build something that was powerful for an internal customer by embracing diversity, and imperative to the external customer in order to feel that level of empathy and understanding. I felt extremely confident in how I would be able to assemble one dynamic that would take roughly six hours to achieve.

For this workshop, I decided to create two imaginary cultures: wabi and sabi. Wabi-sabi is a Japanese concept loaded with meaning. Of the many interpretations, there are two that I love the most. First, there is the idea that wabi-sabi changes our perception of the world to such an extent that a chip or a crack in an object, such as a vase, only serves to make it more interesting, with greater meditative value. The second, wabi-sabi speaks to finding beauty within imperfection.

My wabi-sabi workshop was to be about two cultures who find themselves in difficulty trying to understand the other. Unintentionally, they judge, criticize, and reject each other due to differences in traditions, values, respect, gestures, and perception. My idea was to make the diversity culture concepts I would teach the wabis and the sabis during the workshop go viral, so to speak, and have a lasting effect on participants that would then spread throughout the company. I wanted them to remember what they learned as a team, and lean on these lessons when they faced diversity challenges in the workplace. This, I believed, would ultimately lead to success in embracing diversity culture and seeing the world through a new lens.

After a week of long hours at work and little sleep, the day of my presentation arrived. I was well prepared, and excited for my big shot at landing this project. The universe, however, had different ideas. My wife had to go out of town at the last minute for an important meeting of her own, and our babysitter was unable to step in. All my meticulous plans were thrown out the window in the blink of an eye. I couldn't cancel the meeting, and I certainly didn't want to postpone and potentially miss out. I needed to have this presentation ready to take to Spain, no matter what.

Cecile had asked me the previous night if I was ready, to which I had replied that I absolutely was. How could I now tell her that I would now need to have my daughter join me in this meeting? I was left with little choice, and decided the risk was worth it to take my own company to the next level.

I decided to call Cecile, the night before our scheduled presentation.

"Hi, Cecile, it's me, Johnny. I'm going to be bringing my baby daughter with me to our meeting tomorrow, but don't worry, she's part of the presentation."

Against all luck, Cecile laughed and told me to bring her on in.

Now, my daughter, Chiara, was only sixteen months old at the time. As soon as Cecile gave the okay for her to be with me, I panicked. What if she started shouting? Or wants her bottle? Or dirties her diaper and perfumes the room? Or starts getting fussy and I have to interrupt the meeting to tend to her? All the nightmarish yet reasonably probable scenarios started flashing through my mind.

I figured my best strategy for mitigating the unavoidable was to be prepared. Food, check. Extra diapers, check. Bottle, check. I even packed a spare iPad, her favorite games, and a few more dresses, just in case she should need a wardrobe change midpresentation. I arrived thirty minutes early so I could familiarize my daughter with her surroundings, and pleaded with her not to make any messes. I wasn't convinced she understood a single word I said, but I crossed my fingers that she could sense that something big was about to happen and would be on best behavior.

It turns out that Chiara was quite taken with the meeting room, for whatever reason, and spent the majority of my preparation time giggling. Happy baby, happy daddy.

People started filing into the room as the meeting start time grew near, which sent Chiara scurrying under the table with a few colored pencils and her favorite Peppa Pig coloring book.

At last, it was time to begin.

"Hello everyone, and welcome."

I took a deep breath, and gestured toward my daughter, who was still playing under the table.

"This is my assistant, Chiara."

The room full of professionals all looked at my daughter, and I was momentarily reminded of the movie *Baby Boom*, in which Diane Keaton portrays the ultimate career-woman who inherits a baby and has to sort out how to make it work within her high-powered life.

"The reason she is under the table is because she prefers to go unnoticed. She will, however, be taking notes and if, for any reason, you hear strange noises, that's because she's as excited as I am about this presentation I have for you today."

This was met with chuckles throughout the room. Cecile had my back, and poked her head under the table to speak to Chiara in her lilting French accent.

"Okay, princess, don't worry about the noises. We understand your excitement and if your father isn't doing a good job, we'll be bringing you on as back up."

Thankfully, this unconventional introduction created an immediate sense of connection between everyone in the room. And with it, I felt a sense of peace that everything was going to be fine. Chiara's presence and the sound of her crawling under the table, playing in silence, actually boosted my confidence and helped me perform better for that forty-five minutes.

The highlight of the presentation was a video I'd created, meant to convey the message that everyone is born equal. I included film from a moment when my daughter was tasting ice cream for the first time, and how she used facial expressions and gestures to express her happiness. The video represented the power of body language and how kids teach us about understanding emotions and needs through gestures.

You see, kids have a universal nonverbal language. No matter which language they speak, kids are able to understand each other, and play, laugh, and make friends. As they grow, we teach our kids to say hello, smile, and say please and thank you, even if they aren't able to fully communicate in words yet. But we teach them to say no, and to differentiate themselves from others perhaps not expressly, but in the way we interact. Nonverbal language is powerful, and holds key signs for how we've learned to connect and learn about others.

I created the two wabi and sabi cultures for my presentation to teach participants how to read and interpret body language. We must be aware of how our own gestures are received in cultures other than our own, and find a way in which to respect our traditions without upsetting others. For example, some hand gestures are considered harmless in some countries, and highly offensive in others. This awareness teaches us in turn to notice our own body language in uncomfortable circumstances, or when we don't approve of something we are hearing or seeing.

By being intentional with our body language we are able to connect more easily with others, and help them feel comfortable as well. This power of using our body language to express empathy is crucial in a world of diversity.

At last, my presentation was finished. Chiara seemed to sense this completion, and crawled out from under the table and spontaneously began clapping. The whole room started laughing and clapping with her. It was a joyful moment for us all.

"As you can see," I said, "my assistant is ready to close the deal. Are you?"

The meeting lasted for two hours, with my daughter now sitting at the table with the rest of us. Nobody minded at all. In fact, most people were lined up to take turns playing with her.

I ended that meeting beaming in the knowledge that I had a signed contract, and the best assistant ever. I couldn't wait to call my wife and tell her it was Chiara who helped me close the deal.

The lesson learned here is that as a leader, hesitation can be your worst enemy. Imagine if I had cancelled the meeting, or postponed it because of a hiccup in my plans? That hiccup—my daughter's presence—was in fact my greatest asset. I had faith in my abilities to flip a situation from a negative to a positive. It all depends on the perspective from which you choose to view the world.

Hesitation is also an enemy of the customer experience. Too many leaders leave projects on the table, unfinished, due to hesitation. Hesitation goes hand in hand with fear. Fear holds us back, keeping us from taking risks and accepting new challenges, especially if either of the above could potentially put our expertise on the line. The truth is, you don't always need to know how to do everything. You just need to know how to find the answers to any questions you may have.

The starting point is irrelevant. Start anywhere, and focus on the theme. Do the research into the right topics and you will be able to unleash your creativity and find ways to overcome any challenge. You'll be surprised at how your mind is able to create solutions you never thought possible, when you ask it to.

Your customer's experience is like an open field. There are no limits. Each customer is unique, and their level of expectations is unique. In the field of customer experience, you will face challenges regularly, even daily, some of which will be simple to resolve, while others will require your full attention. Don't hesitate to put your team in challenging situations. This is how you will keep the spark of excitement for creating and achieving alive.

Keep in mind, there are times when a hasty decision is not a good idea. There will be instances in which you'll want to pause, take a step back, or reconsider. So how do you tell the difference? How do you know when to blaze forth, and when extra caution would be prudent?

Before you can determine that answer, you need to ask yourself the following questions:

- **What are my goals?** How appropriate and realistic are they for the foreseeable future of my company? Do I have the resources, knowledge, and support to achieve them within a reasonable timeframe?

- **What are the goals I've articulated for my team?** Does my team understand them clearly and perform the actions to move the company forward? Does my team believe they are realistic? What specific feedback has my team given me regarding these goals?
- **What are my top priorities?** What can I do to clarify which business actions are most important now, and which can wait?
- **In what areas do I have expert knowledge?** In what areas do I find myself "inventing" answers just to appear knowledgeable or save face?
- **What potential consequences and risks are involved with the business decisions I am about to make?** Which ones have I investigated thoroughly? Do I understand the consequences and risks well enough to be prepared to face them?
- **What risks have I ignored in the past?** What were the results?

Your answers may require a healthy amount of time and thought, but they will help you build the awareness and confidence needed to make the right decisions for your career. If any of your answers reveal a weakness or area of deficiency in your business, the best thing to do is take a step back and reconsider your next course of action.

First, you'll want to rally those around you whom you most trust to give you the most honest and helpful feedback.

For example, I come up with at least one new idea every day, an idea that will potentially have a big impact on my business success. Before I make a single move toward executing the idea, I share it with my wife. I love this process, and I hate this process, at the same time.

I hate it because she has the ability of making me consider a question that I hadn't asked myself before. When I sort out my answers to those questions, I realize that my idea was too vague. She helps me see the angles that are missing that would make my idea great.

For most of us, when we have a new idea, we immediately think it's fantastic, and we are immediately excited about it. By sharing your ideas with a person you trust who can give you constructive feedback without poo-pooing your enthusiasm, you are opening yourself to another angle. Often this outside perspective helps you see what's missing that would take your idea from good to great. It's through this feedback process that we avoid hesitation.

We don't necessarily like it when someone tells us our idea doesn't work. We feel like they are destroying our imaginations. But if you are truly someone who wants to take your ideas to the next level, you'll ask for this feedback because you genuinely want to know the answers. You must then accept the critique or opinion given with an open mind.

Make sure to find the right person to ask for this feedback, and make sure that you consider this person to be better than you at certain skills. This person should be someone who is able to add value to your idea, or maybe even present you with a better one.

Q uestions

Are you willing to move your business, your department, or yourself forward for growth? I hope your answer is yes. What actions are you taking on a daily basis? Write down four actions that encourage you to do this every day and those actions will help you achieve your goal and grow professionally.

Are you suffering from lack of diversity culture at your organization? If yes, how do you handle it? How do you embrace diversity? Write down at least four ideas of how you do it or plan to do it.

Have you ever hesitated to make a decision and, as result of your actions, lost an opportunity for growth? When did this happen? What did you learn from it?

Culture and customer experience are inextricable. Culture determines how you design customer experiences, while customer experiences help you sustain culture.

8

Learn What It Takes to Make Your Customers Happy

If you're anything like me, you wake up each morning more happy about your smartphone being charged to 100 percent than you are about the sun peeking up over the horizon. You probably check your phone first, scroll through any notifications you may have missed overnight, and only after you've had your tech fix do you greet your family and start your day.

Chances are during your morning scroll you came across more than a few brands promoting their happy customers and reputation for great customer service. But is "great customer service" really enough these days? The answer is no—it's an expectation for today's customer, not a differentiator. So what's the secret to standing out, and making customers so happy that they choose to buy from you again and again?

There are five essential behaviors that you and every member of your team must master in order to ensure your customers' happiness, and deep satisfaction with the value of what you offer:

- **Be informed.** Learn the profile of your customer, as well as your competitors, and what you can offer that will set you apart. Learn what will amaze anyone who buys from you by getting to know your ideal client well.

- **Be creative and innovative.** Find new ways of doing things that will differentiate you from your competition. Explore hidden details, and offer the unexpected. Being different is always more effective than simply being the best. Creativity and innovation are the fuel that will propel your business to the top and keep it there.
- **Meet expectations.** Meeting your customers' expectations is the first step to exceeding them at every touchpoint by incorporating the differentiating details that will amaze.
- **Be open-minded.** Don't get caught up by in-house rules or the status quo. Consider every demand, and find a way to say yes, even if you have to bend the rules. Having an open mind will help you close any deal quicker, and more directly.
- **Be a doer.** Being a doer is the result of being informed, creative, innovative, able to meet expectations, and open-minded. By being a doer, you will carry any goal through to its completion, and you will have happy customers. It's imperative that everyone at your organization become a doer.

In this chapter, I will share two stories that illustrate how these five behaviors play an important role in making your customer happy.

A Wedding Negotiation

Suzan was set to be married in June 2016. In early May, the sales manager for my hotel, Elisabeth, called me.

"Johnny, Suzan would like to speak with you. She met you in the Dominican Republic at the Hotel Paradisus Punta Cana in 2004. She said you organized her family dinner for New Year's Eve," Elisabeth explained to me, "She has booked fifty rooms for four nights at the Hotel Paradisus in the Dominican Republic again, this time to celebrate her wedding."

Elisabeth went on to say that Suzan had learned that I had been transferred to a sister property in Mexico, and was willing to cancel her wedding in the Dominican Republic and hold it at our property in Cancún—but only if I was in charge of all organization, and we could offer better prices than competitors, whom Suzan was already well-informed on and had negotiated prices and packages with before reaching out to us. However, if we were able to close this deal, we would reach and even achieve our revenue goals for that month. Elisabeth warned me to expect negotiations on price, as Suzan knew that selling a fifty-room block is a great deal for any hotel, especially in June.

"Alright, Elisabeth, send me the conditions you already negotiated with her, what our competitors are currently doing, and the added values you offered her," I said.

"Added values?"

"How did you show her that we're great at what we do, and why she should choose us over our competitors? What did you offer her that made her think wow, I love what they're offering me? What are those small details that will make the difference? Let's forget that she knows me from before, and build an experience that will truly amaze her."

"Um, I offered her the master suite at no charge, with breakfast included, as well as an in-room massage for two, VIP status, and champagne and chocolate-covered strawberries upon arrival as a welcome amenity."

I wasn't wowed by this, and I doubted Suzan was either.

"Elisabeth, these are standard perks given by every hotel, as part of the package. We need to think above and beyond, to how we can add value that will knock her socks off and at the same time won't blow our budget, and we'll land this deal for sure."

Elisabeth told me she was meeting with the wedding planner, and that if I had time the three of us could build an offer together. I was all in.

First, we needed to be informed. I wanted us to understand her needs, ideas, and demands, and brainstorm ways to surprise and delight her when she hears what we have planned.

I tried to remember Suzan from our meeting in the Dominican Republic. I couldn't recall much. So we searched for her on Facebook, and I sent her a friend request. She accepted, and we immediately had access to photos from her holidays with her family, and that New Year's Eve at the Paradisus Hotel. By scouting through her pictures we were able to create a report about her vacation at our sister property, and examine the details to help us get to know her better.

We could see her style, and the way she dresses. The lifestyle she and her family enjoy. We even made notes on the types of drinks she was holding in the pictures, and the kind of food she was eating. We pulled up pictures of her with her boyfriend, but we wanted to confirm she was engaged to this same man before we acted on any ideas.

I asked Elisabeth if it was possible to reduce the price any more, or if we'd reached our limit. She explained to me that there was another group that had booked fifty-seven rooms the same date as Suzan's wedding, and for the same price we had offered her. A 20 percent discount was already included in our offer to Suzan, as well as the master suite free of charge, while the other group would have four rooms upgraded to an ocean view. It was this group's second year staying at our property, and we couldn't risk their business by giving Suzan a different price. It was a dilemma, but it made sense as we could potentially lose both clients.

We need to be creative, innovative… and do something no other hotel was doing. And in order to create a strategy that would include the wow factors we wanted, we needed to speak with Suzan and learn more about what she had in mind.

"Hello, Suzan, this is Johnny, from ME Cancún."

"Johnny, thank you for calling me! I'm so excited for my wedding in June."

"I can imagine you are! I was married four years ago, and it was such a beautiful and emotional experience I'd do it over and over again if I could."

She surprised me by asking if she could ask me a personal question. I said absolutely, ask away. She asked me how it felt to be married, and if I like being settled into married life. I explained that my wife and I had already been living together for eight years before getting married. That we had traveled the world, both of us being in the hotel industry. I said that marriage made our relationship even better, because we learned more about each other and always tried to have fun, no matter what.

She asked if it's true that love fades after the wedding, to which I replied that in reality, love begins when two people accept each other fully, the good and the bad, which doesn't have to change just because they get married.

Suzan went on to explain to me that she met her fiancé, Brian, in high school, and that he was the only boyfriend she'd had. And she was his first girlfriend. She had a fear that Brian might one day get bored, and decide that he wants to meet other women.

"Or you'll get bored with him and want to meet other men," I joked.

"You're right," she laughed.

Kidding aside, I told her that marriage was like a game—sometimes you win, and sometimes you lose. The key is to play the game smart and keep it going, with both partners on the same team finding ways to win. Not that I am a marriage expert, per se, but this had been my experience.

We spoke a bit longer, and then she thanked me for my insights.

Can you identify what was happening between Suzan and I at this moment? She was showing that she trusted me, and I was doing the same for her. We were building a relationship through open conversation. A relationship with your customer is the first step to designing an experience for that person.

During that call, Suzan went on to explain that she received the offer for fifty rooms from Elisabeth, but she felt the price was still too high. She said that competitors were offering a lower price, with the same value-adds, such as breakfast included. She asked if there was anything more I could do, since she wanted to book the rooms that day and celebrate her wedding at our hotel.

I told her I understood her position, and shared my belief that our hotel matched her lifestyle, and the level of service and facilities made it the place to be in Cancún.

For Suzan, it all came down to price, and she was bargaining hard. I knew it would be a tough negotiation. A strong relationship wouldn't be enough to overcome her objections to the cost, but it would help both her and I in maintaining an open mind and listening to the proposal. The relationship, however, wouldn't guarantee that she would buy. My team and I need to come up with an offer she wouldn't be able to refuse.

A stage of objection, as we call it, is not uncommon in any business. This happens when a potential customer loves your product, but balks when it comes time to sign the deal or submit payment.

Often there's a fear of spending the money, or they want to hold out for a better price. Sometimes the customers aren't yet convinced and they feel the need to consult with someone else.

In this case, we knew Suzan's objection was not to the hotel or the wedding package, but to the room price. At our property, it was our philosophy to never use hard-sell tactics, or try to push a sale without offering real additional value. It was our commitment to ensure that each customer was 100 percent willing and excited to spend their money with us, and for us to make every penny 100 percent worth it.

For Suzan, we wanted her to fall in love with what we could offer, and how we make a unique difference in creating a memorable experience for her and her fiancé, and their friends and family, on not only their wedding day, but for each moment the group would be at the hotel.

We needed to show her the value of what we were offering in order to convince her to choose us over our competitors.

This is why the first behavior, being informed, is crucial. By becoming informed, our team was able to gather all the details about Suzan: her social media profile, the price of the other offers she had and what value-adds were included, her lifestyle, her family's lifestyle, and details about her previous New Year's Eve trip to our sister property.

Equipped with this knowledge, we were able to create a scenario which we felt would make Suzan's objection to cost all but vanish.

But first, I needed to make sure the man we saw in those New Year's Eve photos were in fact the man she was set to marry.

"Did I have the pleasure of meeting your fiancé when you stayed with us in the Dominican Republic?"

"Yes, indeed, you did meet him. Brian, the tall guy who was with me on that trip."

Excellent. In preparation for this call, my team had arranged for something unexpected: a live virtual walkthrough of the property. We knew we needed to be creative and innovative, and this was the best solution we could come up with given our short time frame.

"Suzan, are you in front of your computer?"

"Yes, I am."

"Do you have some time now? I would love to walk you through the hotel, and let you see for yourself how magical this place can be. Together we'll do a live virtual tour so you can experience a small part of what we can do, and what makes us stand out from the rest of our competitors."

Suzan loved the idea.

"I have all the time in the world. It's my wedding day and I want it to be perfect, just for a better price!" she laughed.

This virtual walkthrough was our first wow factor. It was unexpected by the customer, and something we could leverage to create more surprises as we toured the property with the IT department's fancy camera.

We got everyone connected online, and then began the tour. We started by walking through the hotel, pointing out different features and introducing Suzan to team members as we passed through different parts of the property.

These introductions, our second wow factor, were enhanced by the team's advance warning that this would be happening, so each member knew Suzan was watching them and were informed enough to greet her by name and make her feel welcome. They also mentioned Brian's name in their greetings, increasing the emotional connection for her.

After these introductions, Suzan shared that she felt like she'd know everyone for ages, and like they were welcoming her home. Our intention was successful.

By studying the relationship between Suzan and her fiancé through social media, and combining that knowledge with what Elisabeth had gathered when presenting the initial offer, we were able to paint a pretty clear picture of them as a couple and their lifestyle, and use that information to meet and exceed expectations.

But we weren't finished yet. Our third wow factor featured a bottle of Veuve Clicquot rosé—her drink of choice as pictured in many of Suzan's Facebook photos—placed in the living room of the master suite. With it was a note that read, "Bubbles for you to remember those moments spent together at the Paradisus for NYE 2004." This scene was the first thing Suzan saw when we entered the suite with our camera.

"Wow, I *love* Veuve Clicquot, and rosé even more! You are the best!" she said excitedly, clapping her hands in admiration for our attention to detail.

Still, we weren't finished. Earlier we had printed a photo of Suzan and Brian that we'd found on Facebook (this was why I confirmed it was in fact the same man I had met), framed it, and had it placed in the master suite bedroom next to the bed. This was the second scene that greeted Suzan during her virtual walkthrough of the master suite, and our fourth wow factor.

Suzan noticed the photo through the screen, and was instantly emotional.

"You know, Johnny, that photo was taken right after Brian popped the question. I absolutely love that photo," she shared with me, tears in her eyes.

Our team had known this, owing to our efforts to be informed ahead of time. The comments on the Facebook post showed us that this particular image was special to the couple.

For the fifth wow factor, we had written a message in golden marker on the mirror of the master suite bathroom. It read, "It is the happiest day of my life. I am getting married today."

"When you are getting ready for the happiest day of your life, you will look in the mirror and see just how happy you are," I explained to her.

"Oh, I just love it," Suzan replied.

"Suzan, would you like to have a personal message from you written on the mirrors in all your friends' and family's fifty rooms each night?"

"That would be amazing, Johnny."

"Consider it done."

It required support of every department involved in this virtual experience to make it a success, which meant that each team member needed to show up with an open mind and a willingness to step outside the box. This collaborative effort brought Suzan's vision for her dream wedding to life, eliciting tears of joy from our potential customer.

Why is keeping an open mind essential for customer experience design? Because as the designer, you are often tasked with presenting projects that require different departments to move out of their comfort zone, and try something that's outside the status quo. Without each team member being open and all in on new ideas, your customer experience design will fail.

Our sequence of wows was designed to amaze. We continued the virtual tour from the master suite on to the wedding venue. We had set up the gazebo where the wedding and dinner would take place, complete with dinner tables arranged on the beach with white and gold tablecloths and a chandelier so Suzan could envision how it would be on the big day. Suzan's smile and tears of joy made every minute behind these efforts worth it.

Afterward, Suzan shared how much this virtual walkthrough meant to her.

"Johnny, you cannot imagine how happy I feel at this moment," she said. "If I was at your hotel, I would hug your whole team. It is exactly how I want it. You've made it easy for me, and are making my dream a reality."

By first creating a unique experience, and then demonstrating the value behind our offer, Suzan was more willing to say yes to the location and close the deal.

But remember, it was price that was the original objection, not the property itself. It was our ability to create the perception of high value that dissolved this objection, paving the way for us to secure the group.

If a potential customer can perceive the value behind an offer, then the chances of success over objections increase exponentially. Winning over objections is not enough, however. We also need to address the sense of guilt over spending that amount of money.

I explained to Suzan that by choosing us over our competitors, she would actually be saving money, not paying more. The added values would delight every single guest, making them happy they chose to travel and join her on her special day, and be there for such a memorable experience. And of course the guarantee of the highest level of service goes without saying.

I pointed out that what she was doing was investing in an exceptional wedding day, and an outstanding stay at the hotel. Before she gave me an answer though, I promised that what she saw on the live virtual tour and what my sales manager and colleague, Elisabeth, offered will be our compromise with you. I told her that if she put her happiest day in our hands, we will exceed her expectations.

"Now more than ever I know why we followed you to Cancún," Suzan said to me. "I have just one condition, I want you to enjoy my wedding, and it would be lovely if your wife could join us as well."

"I will enjoy your wedding," I laughed, "and will try to bring my wife too."

All that was left to do was to close the deal.

"Elisabeth is with me right now, and she is sending you the contract, Suzan. You will see in the agreement that I will be supporting Elisabeth as a wedding planner, as requested."

"I do have one last favor," I added. "I am supposed to be on holiday with my family the exact week of your wedding, but I promised you I would be there to toast to your lifetime of happiness. Please do sign the contract within 24 hours so I know whether or not to change the dates for our family vacation."

Suzan signed in less than one hour.

Our team used all five behaviors—be informed, be innovative and creative, meet expectations, be open-minded, and be a doer —to successfully close this deal with Suzan and ensure our customer was happy.

The wedding was an extraordinary success, enjoyed by all who attended, and most of all by the happy couple, who couldn't imagine having hosted their special day anywhere else.

A Desperate Customer

This particular story happened in March 2018, and it's one I often use as an example in keynote talks and training workshops when speaking about how to make a customer happy.

I was traveling to New York City, and after a late arrival time checked in at the NoMad New York at 11:00 at night. I had a conference the next day with one hundred people who were there to learn about enhancing the customer experience. It was set to start at 7:30 in the morning.

In accordance with Murphy's Law, when I got to my room I noticed that the charger for my laptop had been damaged somehow. And, of course, my battery was almost dead. I was in a panic, as I had yet to rehearse my presentation for the final time, and I needed my computer for the conference the next morning.

With my stress mounting, I called reception.

"Hi, this is Johnny, in Room 305. Do you know if anyone at the hotel would have a power cord for a MacBook Pro so I can charge my laptop?"

"We're very sorry, sir, but unfortunately not."

"Do you know of any store then that might be open at this time of night where I could buy one?"

"No, the first store where you can buy anything for your Mac will not be open until 10:00 tomorrow morning."

I was really starting to panic now. I used the last bit of juice my battery had to search for any electronics store that would be open at midnight, and presto! I discovered the Apple Store on 5th Avenue was open 24/7.

I immediately ran downstairs to flag a taxi, and arrived outside the store where one of the Apple employees was greeting customers.

"Good evening, how may I assist you?"

"I need a power cord for my MacBook Pro for an event I have tomorrow morning. Can you help me?"

"Absolutely, let me assign you to one of my associates inside who will assist you with your purchase."

"Also, our DJ, Andrew, is playing chill out music until 2:00 a.m.," my Apple savior added, "so after you complete your purchase please join us for a complimentary glass of champagne."

Who could say no to that treatment?

I was so thrilled with the way the Apple Geniuses treated me that night, and for being so open and willing to resolve my situation, that I ended up staying at the store sipping champagne and dancing until the music ended. I completely forgot about my final rehearsal, first in the drama in tracking down a new power cord, and then in the elation of having my problem solved.

The next morning at the conference, I put aside the material I had prepared for my keynote talk, and instead shared this story. I asked the audience if they knew there was an Apple store in the city that was open twenty-four hours. Of the hundred attendees, only fifteen knew about this.

This story demonstrates the power of being informed in enhancing your customer experience and delighting customers with your level of service. Imagine if the staff at my hotel had been well informed, not only about what is going on at their own property, but also what's available in the city that might benefit their guests.

Approximately 75 percent of guests staying at NoMad New York are business travelers. What if they had made a list of all the requests their guest might make, and all the needs they might have, and equipped reception with prepared solutions and information? Do you think that would impress guests? Absolutely it would!

How would my experience have been that night if they already had an extra power cord available at reception? Would that have made me as the customer happy? I can assure you, I would have been over the moon.

Or how might I have felt if the receptionist who answered my desperate call allayed my panic by responding differently. He could have told me not to worry, that New York never sleeps, and that there is an Apple store in the city that is open twenty-four hours a day, seven days a week. She could have offered to call me a cab so I could get there faster. And if she had been truly informed, she could have told me about the DJ and champagne.

That would have taken my happiness as a customer to the next level.

But imagine if the receptionist went further still, and called me shortly after to follow up, and ensure that my problem was solved.

That person could say something along the lines of, "Hello, Mr. Sfeir, my name is Jonathan and I am stepping in to make sure everything is solved. I have already sent a message to our IT team, who will be arriving before 7:00 a.m., to see if anyone has a power cord for a MacBook Pro that they could lend you. I see also that you do not currently have a wake-up call scheduled— please let me know if you would like an alarm set."

That would have been truly exceptional. Would you return to a hotel who demonstrated this level of service? Would you become a loyal patron of that brand owing to the outstanding attention to detail? Would you be happy with the delivery of service?

Absolutely you would! That level of service is impeccable, and will amaze customers with the efficiency and preparation. They may be surprised at how well-informed reception is, and how willing they are to please guests. No doubt they will become an ardent brand ambassador based on the feelings you were able to inspire.

Keeping customers happy is not just a platitude, it's an essential component to the success of your business. Do not underestimate or overlook its potential to skyrocket your brand.

Questions

What is your current strategy for making your customers happy? Write down at least five examples.

Do you encourage employees to think differently? How? Mention at least three ways.

Do you believe your business team is well informed about what is going on at your company and community? How do you get them told?

Do you establish a creative and innovative climate? How do you encourage creativity and innovation?

Do you reward the doers? If so, how?

Actions to Take

By implementing a new behavior strategy into your organization, you will become a very effective customer experience designer, and for sure a happy customer is the result of it. Those five behaviors helped me close big deals in many different businesses and negotiations:

• Being informed

• Being creative and innovative

• Meeting expectations

• Being open-minded

• Being a doer

Build your behavioral concept, and you will be surprised by the understanding and outstanding results you will have at your business.

Design customer experiences from the inside of your company out. Internal customers supply the fuel you need to survive. External customers supply the voice you need to thrive.

9

HYPE-HOP Your Way through Customer Experience Design

I am always trying to HYPE-HOP by way through life, and through my role as a customer experience designer, in order to create a collection of memorable moments. So, what does HYPE-HOP mean?

The HYPE refers to the *hyped-up energy* required to design your customer experience. The HOP refers to the actions you take to execute your plan, and celebrate the results:

- HYPE your gratitude to HOP your happiness.

- HYPE your smile to HOP your attitude.

- HYPE your knowledge to HOP your growth.

- HYPE your Monday to HOP your weekend.

- HYPE your creativity to HOP your success.

- HYPE your discipline to HOP consistency.

- HYPE your passion to HOP your confidence.

Whenever I work with a management team, I let them know when it's time to HYPE-HOP. Once the team members understand what I am asking them to do, they begin to pass this practice down to their own teams. Eventually, as it spreads, you'll hear team members shouting at each other, "Come on, let's HYPE to be able to HOP" all over the resort. They encourage each other to make things happen, and forget the amount of time it takes or the level of effort behind it. Let's HYPE-HOP together through each of these principles.

HYPE Gratitude to HOP Your Happiness

As a human, you naturally seek the feeling of happiness. But have you ever considered the possibility that in *seeking* happiness you lose the opportunity to actually experience the feeling? When we rush through life in search of the next best thing, we forget to look at what already exists in our lives that can make us happy. We stop appreciating the little things in life.

Each moment, if we are present and actively engaged rather than worrying about the past or future, is an opportunity for play. Gratitude is the key to unlocking this secret of life.

I learned the value of gratitude intimately as a youth growing up in Lebanon. I was twelve years old when the civil war broke out, living with my family as refugees in a tiny space in Baabdat, a small Christian village where everyone knew each other. It was a challenging time, and the country very quickly ran out of electricity, potable water, and other such daily essentials.

By that time, schools had also closed, and we children were left with the freedom to fill our days however we chose. We passed the time playing a game that involved running around to look for metal that had been left behind by the bombs the night before, and then using it to create art objects, like a vase, figurines, or a key holder. In spite of being surrounded by danger and uncertainty, we used our creativity to transform these deadly weapons into something beautiful. We even went so far as to advertise our creations and sold them to other villagers for twenty-five piastres, which was around twenty-five cents.

As time passed, people got used to living without electricity and turned to candles or diesel lanterns to light their homes. We had no need for heat or hot water during the summer months, but winter in this mountainous terrain is extremely tough. Heating was essential, as even a few days without warmth in the home can be deadly.

The villagers had started using wood stoves in their homes to keep from freezing, as well as to cook food and even shower. But during the day, the stove wasn't an option. A clear blue sky meant that any enemy troops on a nearby mountain would be able to see the smoke and know to target us for their next bombing. The only times we could use our stoves was at night, right before bed, and never under a full moon.

Finding potable water was another challenge. Again, safety was a primary concern, and we'd have to wait and gauge when it would be least risky to leave our homes and be outside. Then it would take two hours to reach the nearest fountain unless we wanted to draw water from the sink, boil it, and add drops of lemon in order to avoid contracting cholera.

For food, we had limited supplies of bread and rice. We were lucky to get some form of meat or chicken once a week. Depending on the season, we could find plenty of fruit on the mountain, including peaches, apples, oranges, and grapes. I never experienced hunger during this period though, as my parents reserved most of the hearty, nutritious meals for us kids and made them do themselves with little more than soup. This fact we didn't even realize until we were told many years later.

The truth is, during this troubled time I could never shake the fear of sudden death. It always seems to be dark, and cold for at least half the year. The sound of bombs exploding in the village was a constant thrum, and our house shook like paper. The only thing that made us feel even remotely safe was when my mom would cover us with mattresses for protection.

Years later, when the electricity and hot water returned, I began to realize how periods of loss, danger, and scarcity can make a person grateful for all of life's blessings. It felt amazing to flip a switch and light up a room, turn a knob and shower with hot water, eat full meals, and drink water that wouldn't make me sick. I understood that the most important blessings were simply opening my eyes each morning and taking in the light of day, and having parents who loved me.

Any time these memories come up, I HYPE my gratitude for family, for every day, for my friends, a job I love, my customers who bring me business, as well as for the insights and creativity to write this book and all of the readers engaging with it. Gratitude for all of this means I am happy, and that I have many things to celebrate and enjoy.

I share these stories at every opportunity so that my teammates and associates can HYPE their gratitude as well, and together we can HOP positive energy to our customers and deliver incredible experiences.

HYPE Your Smile to HOP Your Attitude

We've all looked in the mirror at some point and thought, "I look ugly today." We've then sought confirmation from friends, family, or a partner. As soon as you cross paths with someone, you ask, "I look awful today, right?" Then comes the rebuttal, "Don't be stupid. You look great."

It doesn't matter that the feedback was positive. You've already convinced yourself that your face has changed drastically, that you've visibly aged in twenty-four hours or some other line is on your forehead that you hadn't seen before. You create an energy that's not overtly negative, but it's not exactly positive either. Your attitude is neutral, which worsens your self-image. And this blah state of mind is what you will project with every word, and every gesture, as you go about your day.

People ask you, "Are you okay? You look very serious today."

"Yes, I'm fine," you reply, denying that you're not really okay, and further darkening your mood from blasé to bordering on angry. All the while you're strengthening this conviction that your face *really does* look older, or uglier, and it makes it more and more difficult for you to smile.

You don't need me to tell you that HYPE-ing your smile will provide an instant boost, and is exactly the drug you need to lift your mood and transfer that positive energy to everyone around you.

A smile is what opens doors, and attracts people to you, making everything easier. Your smile and the energy attached to it has the potential to be contagious and lift the spirits of everyone around you.

But what does this mean for your role as a customer experience designer? It means that your smile is a key indicator of the energy you are putting out there, both to your associates and to your customers. It's far too easy to fall into a daily routine and forget to smile. Little by little as the daily drudgery goes on, you begin to frown and before long you're scowling at everyone and everything. This is not the energy you must operate from to create a successful customer experience.

Here's a quick tip for when I forget to smile. When I find myself frowning, I unlock one of my devices—my phone or my laptop, whichever is on hand—and look at the images I've saved on the screens. I purposefully choose images that always make me smile. Often, it's a photo of my daughter. Whenever I see her face smiling back at me from the screen, I absorb that positivity, and I know that I will be able to extend that attitude to my customers.

Giving your customer a sincere smile is one of the most important and effective ways to immediately enhance the customer experience. Your attitude will be contagious, and you'll often find that the people surrounding you will smile right back.

HYPE Your Knowledge to HOP Your Growth

I remember my father always saying, "We are born in a classroom, and we will die in a classroom." This sounded awful when I was young, but as I grew older I realized what he meant is that active learning drives knowledge, and knowledge drives growth. How are we able to continue to grow and evolve if we aren't constantly learning?

Whether you're just starting out in your career or are advancing up through the ranks, you must continue to build knowledge. Each place, and each situation, can act as your classroom. Invest in these opportunities and watch your confidence blossom.

Participants in my workshops often ask me where I get my ideas. My answer is always the same. I am always in a classroom, learning new market trends and opening my mind to how I can improve at what I do.

Remember to ask yourself, "Can I get better at what I do?" If the answer is that you're unsure, then I'd encourage you to find new opportunities until you find one that allows ample room for improvement, rather than just coasting. When you answer yes to that question, it's a poignant sign that you love what you do. It means your heart is in it, and your mind is looking for ways to go deeper into your industry and master the skills required.

The next question to ask is whether or not you are investing time in self-improvement, and what efforts are you willing to make in order to be the best.

When I first started my company I had a goal to master online marketing strategies. I found a degree I could complete at Cornell University and dove it. I had a bit of knowledge going in, so I thought it would be easy peasy. It certainly wasn't. But I stuck with it, and the effort I put in made both the personal challenge and the time and money invested worth every second and cent.

Always prepare yourself and your teams for improvement. You cannot fall behind the trends of your market and what your competitors are doing. If you stay behind, your customers' experience will be affected, and they will go elsewhere to get what they want. This is true for not only your external customers but the internal ones as well. Training fuels you and motivates you to perform on the job, and this energy will transfer to your team.

HYPE Your Monday to HOP Your Weekend

Why do we always complain about Monday? Why are we already feeling stressed on a Sunday night in anticipation of Monday? Because on Monday:

- You decide to start your diet.
- You decide to change your attitude and be nicer to your mother-in-law.
- You decide to look for a new job.
- You want to work on your faith.
- You start at the gym.
- Winter feels colder than other days.
- Everyone is serious.

Because leading up to Monday, people say things like:

- "I'll give you the answer on Monday."

- "Come in for an interview on Monday."

- "Let's find a solution on Monday."

- "Let's talk on Monday."

- "I will call you on Monday."

- "Visit my office on Monday."

- "Return on Monday."

- "I want it done on Monday."

- "Please remind me on Monday."

- "Your exams begin on Monday."

Here's what never happens on Monday, because no one is in a festive mood:

- Sex

- A haircut

- Happy hour

As children, we learn from our parents that Monday is a stressful day to be dreaded.

"Okay, time for bed," your mother says. "Tomorrow's Monday and I'm going to drop you off at school early so I can get a jump on my work week."

The next morning, you're waiting outside the school for two hours before it opens. It's still dark, and cold. You're sleepy and standing there wishing it were any other day besides Monday. You'd give anything for it to be Sunday, but then you change your mind because Sunday would mean Monday comes next, and that's no good.

You then grow up, and every weekend you waste energy and sacrifice joy by thinking about what's going to happen when the workweek starts all over again.

And if Mondays were a day off? The same thing happens, only we'd think of Tuesday with the same level of stress that we currently apply to Monday.

If you dread Monday, consider how your customers might feel. They probably hate it too. The last place they want to be is at work performing boring tasks. The second last place they want to be is receiving a service from someone who conveys nothing but negative emotions.

"How are you doing, sir?"

"Fine, and you?"

"Okay, just one of those Mondays."

"Yeah, don't you wish it was the weekend again?

This is no way to start your week.

As customer experience designers, we must HYPE about Monday, almost to the point of exaggeration. That way, instead of creating an experience that both us and our customers dread, we create a Monday full of surprises that spark creativity and joy. This is the only way you will HOP up your customers' experience with you, and your level of success.

HYPE Your Creativity to HOP Your Success

Creativity is crucial for the success of any customer experience project. Every time a client asks me to design a personalized workshop or to consult with them, I make sure that I master these three states of mind:

- **Curiosity** is the 360-degree angle of the business. Being curious means having the mental drive to understand the needs and vision of your customer. How does your customer's market behave? What are competitors doing or *not* doing? By starting with curiosity and asking these questions, you can make each project your best work.
- **Connection** means being self-aware and seeking ways to engage customers' attention and trust and to establish a friendship. It's not enough to create something wonderful if you cannot connect with your customer.
- **Courage** means overcoming the disappointment that past failures leave behind, and the fear that you'll repeat a failure so that you can present new ideas with confidence.

When you master these states of mind, you will unleash your creativity and HOP up your success. Creativity is not about thinking outside of the box. Rather, it's about building a new box that differentiates you and your customers from others in your industry. You can generate ideas by:

- Changing your scenery.
- Observing your surroundings: the colors, sounds, words, gestures, people, everything you can see, feel, hear, and perceive.

- Taking notes of all your thoughts.
- Projecting your findings visually on a wall or big screen.

HYPE Your Discipline to HOP Consistency

Think about a moment when you wanted to achieve a specific goal, but you lacked the discipline to reach the finish line. You felt disappointed, right? You'd built up all these expectations for what success would look like, then, you failed to achieve it.

Or think about when you've been a customer and you had an expectation about your experience that wasn't met. That feeling of disappointment, either because you didn't achieve your goal or because a company did not meet your standards, is what we want to avoid as customer experience designers.

Your mission is to exceed those expectations—your own and those of your customers. To do this, you need discipline and consistency in your life and your profession.

Let's consider, for a moment, the discipline required to be a runner. Even just to participate in a race, a runner must train consistently leading up to the event. To place first, second, or third, a runner must train harder and longer year-round. Marathoners, for example, stay in shape at all times and don't understand the meaning of the words *off-season*. Come rain, sleet, snow, or shine, a runner's shoes are on their feet, and those feet are pounding the pavement—faster, longer, better, stronger.

Delivering great customer service works the same way, minus the running shoes. Every day, you must repeat high-impact actions and tasks that lead to success. No lapse in activity. No waiting for motivation to come to you. You must provide your own motivation. Consistent actions give you a better understanding of what you offer, how you offer it, and what you can do to innovate new solutions.

The lesson? Keep doing what works, but never sleep on it. Keep innovating to take what works to the next level.

When you HOP up consistency, you can achieve any goal and celebrate at all times.

HYPE Your Passion to HOP Your Confidence

Customer experience designers must love what they do, and believe without a doubt that the world needs what they have to offer. A strong desire to serve customers is imperative. Many of us have this desire. We don't doubt our orientation toward hospitality. But do we feel confident?

The trick is to explore all your passions.

One characteristic I've noticed about myself is that I don't fixate on a single passion. I don't enjoy getting stuck on one idea, because it means I lose the opportunity to transform and grow. My passions for customer experience, for life, and for learning increase when I make time to explore new ideas and add new components to old interests.

Following your passions might be tricky, but doing something you love *with* passion will open more doors, especially in hospitality, where it's tied so closely with the value you're creating for the customer.

For example, in March 2019, I was in charge of rebranding a hotel in Barcelona. On the last day of training, there was a party for hotel staff so they could enjoy the facilities and get a taste for the food and beverage experience. The host of the party was an account manager named Diego.

Have you ever encountered an accounting manager who was also an entertainer? In all my twenty-two years as a hotelier, Diego was the first I'd come across.

Before the party, Diego came to me and said, "I have to rehearse, I am so nervous."

"You will be fine," I replied. "Just be yourself and you'll build confidence. If you forget anything, don't worry, the audience doesn't know your script anyway."

Diego amazed everyone when he went on stage that night, including himself.

After his performance when he exited the stage, he approached me.

"You know, Johnny, I thought I had found my passion a long time ago. But the fact is, I love to communicate my know-how in front of people the way I did tonight on stage."

Hospitality has an incredibly wide range of opportunities in which to deliver service to customers. But for so long, Diego's passion was for accounting, and he remained stuck in those tasks. Now that he's been exposed to a world outside of numbers, Diego has expanded his newly found passion into becoming a keynote speaker on improving service and motivating the staff to become better at what they do.

Don't get stuck in one passion. Look for multiple avenues to deliver great service, and expand your passions to include them all.

Questions

Review these questions with your team, then have them share their answers and learn from others:

- What are you grateful for?
- How often do you smile during the course of a day? What do you do to keep a smile on your face? What can you count on to make you smile?
- What do you do to educate yourself on new approaches and educate and prepare your teams to execute your vision?
- What are your thoughts about Monday and your behaviors on the first day of the workweek?
- What sparks your creativity?
- In what ways can everyone be creative?
- In what areas of your personal and professional life are you most disciplined and consistent?
- What is your secret for being so disciplined?
- What gets you out of bed every morning?
- What motivates you to keep going throughout the day and the week?
- What activities help you get through challenges?
- What do you do to teach yourself more about what you are passionate about?
- How does this increase your confidence?
- What do you do to expand your passions?
- Actions to Take
- Make gratitude part of your team philosophy.
- Examine your schedule and task list for ways to be more consistent and disciplined.
- Focus on one major goal at a time. Delegate certain tasks to others.
- Avoid beginning every single new thing on Monday. Use

other days of the week to begin new and important
goals.

- Dump anything that does not move you closer to your
  goal.
- Keep your eyes on the goal even when things become
  difficult with your customers.
- Use the "slow" season as an opportunity to restore your
  energy and improve how you deliver service.
- Always communicate your expectations to every
  employee.
- Teach them the value of excellence and consistency.

Technology helps us win the race against time. Human connection helps us win the race for customers' hearts.

Hope

eople like to say we should never lose hope. They apply this platitude to all aspects of life: stress, pain, even love (or especially love).

As repetitive as it sounds, hope should be on the list of words we use most often. Hope must serve as a guide for our thoughts, our interactions, and our goals. Hope should also serve as a beacon lighting the way through every moment.

So what is hope, exactly? And how do humans experience it? By definition, hope is a state of mind that acts as a magnet for our dreams and desires. It's our brain creating images in our mind's eye that support that belief that yes, what I am imagining *will* become a reality, and yes, whatever you desire will in fact happen. Just as hope guides our thoughts and actions, it also influences our purchasing decisions. This holds true for you, for anyone you know personally, and, most importantly, for the purpose of this book, for your customers.

Do you consider the level of hope your customers may have in their minds before they buy your products, require your services, or experience your brand? Based on all previous answers I've collected when asking this question, I'm going to say no, you have not thought about hope as it relates to your customers.

As a customer experience designer, you must be able to integrate hope into your offerings. Hope is how you achieve empathy, and by establishing this level of connection your customers will become firmly attached to your brand, and more likely to trust you. In this final chapter, I will teach you how to harness the power of your customers' hopes so that you will be able to provide experiences that fulfill their dreams.

As we've done throughout this book, I want you to first think about what it's like to *be* a customer. What do you hope every purchase you make will bring you? How will it change your life for the better?

For example, let's say the holidays are coming and you want to travel with your partner or family to a resort to celebrate the season. You go online to view your options, and finally decide on an all-inclusive package: rooms, activities, dining options—all included in the set price.

What are you hoping for with this vacation? You've been saving money for this trip, and now that you've found a place you start dreaming . . . visualizing all the things you'll do, and how much fun you'll have. You start preparing yourself mentally and physically for an outstanding experience. You're putting in a real effort to be ready, and are excitedly awaiting your departure date.

Your customers have this same sense of anticipation. Whether they buy a holiday package at a resort, a day at the spa, or $2,000 worth of new clothing online, they spend their money with a feeling of hope.

What are they hoping for? For the resort holiday, they're hoping to have a top-quality experience. They hope their families will be delighted during the time spent together. They hope a spa day will bring them peace and relaxation after a stressful week, or that the clothes that are being shipped with make them feel attractive and confident.

Customers will go so far as to visualize every detail, and fantasize about the experience they hope to have, and connect the price tag to that wish. They hope to be shown at they've spent their money on something worthwhile.

We as humans have hopes for everything in our lives, and everything on which we've spent our hard-earned money.

We hope the shirt we bought online fits, and that it matches our pants and looks as flattering on us as it did on the model.

We hope we made the right choice when choosing a school for our kids, one that will provide them with the great education they need for a successful life.

We hope the house we bought will be our dream home.

We hope the new job will be a good fit, and that we'll be able to grow with and enjoy working for the new company.

When we love someone, we hope to be loved in return and to spend the rest of our lives with that person.

When we invest money into anything, we hope that decision proves to be a good one, and that it will support us in achieving our dreams.

And when we dream, we hope that our dreams will come true.

I had a dream. For some time now I've been looking to buy property in Spain, on the island of Mallorca. I wanted a rustic old house that I could fix up and make a home.

After years of searching online, I finally came across a place that felt right. I reached out to the owner, who said he could show me the property within a week's time.

As I waited for this showing, I found myself hoping that this really would be the right place. I began to envision how I would transform this rustic property into my dream home. I could already picture myself living there.

The price was higher than I wanted to spend, so I hoped there was room to negotiate. I wanted this so badly that I dreamt of the house every night. All these hopes and desires and I hadn't even seen the property yet.

Why was I so set on this specific house? It was because of the story in the advertisement.

A normal listing for a house will include the dimensions, a description of how beautiful it is, and all the features that add to the value. This is all standard information, nothing to really pull at the heartstrings.

The property I'd found was different. It told the story behind the house. And it went like this:

My name is Toni, and I am the current owner of this house after inheriting it from my mother in 1962. I come from a humble family of hard workers, with two brothers and three sisters. My father was a farmer, and my mother an English teacher.

We grew up living from the land, never going to the market for any fruit or vegetable, and collecting our own water from the rain. We had no heating system, but we did have a chimney. We used to all curl up in the winter next to it so as to feel its warmth, and listen to stories our mother told us about how our father started building this house with his father in the early 1900s, and how they had felt blessed to be able to be self-reliant. We made everything at home.

We had animals, including a guard dog named Blacky, a rescue my father found on the streets. She was a mutt, but she was a great dog for our family growing up. We didn't have toys, instead playing outside in the forest with Blacky by our side, and helping our dad on the farm. He taught us how to grow fruits and vegetables and even grains organically, without the use of any pesticides or chemical fertilizers.

Our friends would come by on Fridays after school to play, and sometimes spend the weekend. Dad had built a pool for us using rocks from the nearby forest, so it looked like a lake. Us kids delighted in that pool.

His dream was to use this land to build a restaurant that served healthy foods, with small fruit and vegetable trucks where customers could buy fresh produce. He passed away at the age of ninety-four, without having built this vision. He was able to create a space where people could come for lunch, or even celebrate events, such as small weddings, and eat straight from the land.

In the end, it wasn't a question of money when it came to realizing his dream… it was time.

You might wonder with all the emotional connection to this house, why sell it?

Our family members, including my mother, now live 25,000 kilometers away. One of my brothers is a successful lawyer in New York City, and one of my sisters is a teacher at Harvard University in Boston. I myself, along with my mother and my family, now own a bakery in Switzerland.

We wish to sell the property, but not to just anyone. We need to see that you love it as we do, and to feel that you belong in this magical place. If you are aiming to turn it into a modern chalet, this is not the property for you. If you want a project you can invest in, fix up and make a home, this could be a perfect fit.

What struck me about this listing was that the owner, Toni, truly considered the hopes his customer may have. Even though he may not have intentionally had a strategy in mind, he knew how to touch the hearts of his target market. He was looking for people who would feel an emotional connection to the place and transform it while keeping its authenticity.

Whether he knew it or not, he understood my hope and helped me take my vision from a dream to a reality.

Storytelling is a powerful tool for turning your customers' hopes into realities. Without even seeing your product, or experiencing your service, you can invite them into your world and touch their hearts. Use real stories to bring your customers' hopes to life.

Questions

- Have you ever thought about customer hope?
- Have you ever thought about what you hope when you consume a product or a service?
- Have you ever asked your employees what they hope to get from you as a leader?
- Have you ever asked your employees what they hope to become?
- Have you ever asked what your customers hope to find at your business?
- Actions to Take
- Ask your employees about their hopes in all stages.
- Ask your customers about what they hope for when they enter your business.
- Create a hope customer experience strategy, where you build experiences based on the hope of your customers.
- Build a hope customer experience board and let your internal customers share the hopes of your customers after asking them. Focus on positive things; negative hopes bring no good to anyone.
- Think what kind of hope list you can offer at your business to take your customer experience to the next level.

Having more experience or being promoted in your job doesn't mean you are more knowledgeable. You build knowledge in a classroom. It doesn't matter if it is inside class or outside of class the most important thing is that you are always in class.

About the Author

With more than 20 years of experience in the demanding world of hospitality, Johnny Sfeir knows firsthand how story-worthy experiences can elevate a business to become a well-known, well-loved brand. As a noted customer experience designer and public speaker, Johnny's vision is to help hospitality and retail brands as well as corporations achieve greatness by implementing innovative ideas and transformational customer experience techniques.

It is with this mission that Johnny founded both his personal brand, Johnny Sfeir Karam, and his teaching platform, Customer Experience Academy.

Through these ventures, Johnny's talks and training have positively impacted thousands of people around the world, helping to enhance both their personal and professional lives.

Johnny is the author of "Become the Best Version of You," Parts 1 & 2, in which readers first discover how to do an effective self-assessment and create new habits, and then use this foundation to achieve their purpose in life.

He is also the creator of the WABI SABI Simulation, a highly successful training centered around diversity, culture, and Boost! The Idea Booster Game, a fun, daily teamwork game that teaches the power of a positive attitude in up-leveling ideas.

Johnny is also a highly sought-after speaker and teacher, and designer of successful workshop and seminar experiences on topics such as:

- Raising Your Customer Experience to Beyond Excellent
- Team Power in Customer Experience
- Up-Selling & Cross-Selling: Negotiation Using NLP Techniques
- Aligning Body Language with Emotions
- Progression in Customer Experience
- Mastering the Power of Public Speaking
- Without Challenge, There Is No Change

… and more.

On stage, Johnny is high energy, full of enthusiasm, and capable of engaging his audience and creating an emotional connection within seconds. Attendees to his events regularly leave motivated and thirsting for more.

He has conducted more than 500 trainings, workshops, and seminars throughout his career for corporations, hotel chains, universities, retailers, and even the pharmaceutical industry.

Today, Johnny lives in Palma de Mallorca, Spain, and is still traveling the globe while designing revolutionary customer experiences.

To learn more about Johnny Sfeir Karam and his success trainings, Train the Trainer Program, or to inquire about hiring him as a keynote speaker, workshop facilitator, or trainer, you can contact him directly at:

Johnny@cxacademy.es

+34 660 387 004

www.cxacademy.com

https://www.linkedin.com/in/joincxacademy/

Before You Go

It was such an honor to spend time with you throughout your reading of this book. I'd like to take just a few more minutes to make a request. It's not a large one.

If you enjoyed this book, would you be so kind as to take a moment, go to Amazon, and look up the title, "Soul Creations: Designing Exceptional Customer Experiences and Heart-Centric Worthy Lives" and/or type in my name: Jonny Sfeir and, once you arrive on my book's sales page, leave a short review? Even if you only had time to go through a couple of chapters you will be able to leave a review and, if you desire, go back later and add to it once you've had a chance to complete the book. Your first impressions are very useful, so don't worry if you only have time now to review one or two chapters.

Finally, note that books succeed by the kind, generous time readers take to leave honest reviews. This is how other readers learn about books that are most beneficial for them to buy. To this end, I thank you in advance for this very kind gesture of appreciation. It means the world to me.

Acknowledgments

It would not have been possible to write this book without a team of helpers and believers.

SOUL CREATIONS began four years ago, with a conversation with my wife, Vanessa Estaras, when I told her I wanted to share my stories with the world. She replied, "Great! What's stopping you?"

I told her I wasn't a writer, to which she told me I didn't need to be a writer, I just needed a story to tell. She believed that my stories could help others as they've helped me.

Words cannot describe the feelings and gratefulness I have for her. She has always done so much to support me, our daughter, Chiara, and our family, and given so much of herself to others. She is my hero. Thank you, my love, for allowing me to believe that everything is possible. Your soul is present in this book.

I want to acknowledge the people who helped SOUL CREATIONS go from idea to reality–their support makes a difference in my life, and the lives of others.

To my mother, Norma, who always believed in me no matter how crazy my plans appeared to be. My sister, Carole, and her enthusiasm for any project, and her constant presence and support. And my brother, Toni, and his endless display of love.

To my editor, Amy Hayes, who brought my ideas to life through words when I could not, and helped make this project a reality. I am fully grateful. studio.theglobalcreator.com and email: studio@theglobalcreator.com

To the creative mind behind my brand, Enid Nolasco, who introduced me to the right people and provided feedback throughout this project. Thank you. **https://www.therawmade.com/ or email her at** enid@therawmade.com

To Melissa G Wilson, the magic touch who brought all of the pieces together and helped launch SOUL CREATIONS out into the world. I am grateful to how connected we have been through this process, and it has been a wonderful experience working with you. https://www.networlding.com/ or email her at melissa@networlding.com.

I am grateful to Melia Hotels International for offering me so many opportunities to try out. The variety of positions and tasks helped me become who I am today.

To all my friends, family, family Sfeir and Estaras, thanks for being the shoulder I can always depend on.

And to all my customers, who have shown me the potential behind my stories and how they can impact others in both their personal and professional lives.

SOUL CREATIONS is not only a collection of stories, but also the essence behind each anecdote that has made me the best version of myself.

Printed in Poland
by Amazon Fulfillment
Poland Sp. z o.o., Wrocław

89585982R00115